CarbSmart®
Grain-Free, Sugar-Free Living Cookbook

50 AMAZING LOW-CARB & GLUTEN-FREE RECIPES FOR YOUR HEALTHY KETOGENIC LIFESTYLE

Dana Carpender

Caitlin Weeks, NC

Edited by Marcy Guyer

CarbSmart Press

A Division of CarbSmart, Inc.

CarbSmart.com

"*People of Grain-Free-Sugar-Free-Land Rejoice! The end of deprivation is here! Dana and Caitlin offer culinary freedom—from the tyranny of grains and sugar. Enjoy ketchup & steak sauce, once more. Eat pie, crackers. Heck, let them eat cake! Thanks to their amazing recipes, emancipation from toxic sugar and gluten is no longer a dream!*"

—Susie T. Gibbs, Writer and Photographer
Fluffy Chix Cook, fluffychixcook.com

"*The legendary Dana Carpender does it again, this time in company with Paleo nutritionist and fitness expert Caitlin Weeks. A collection of simple and straightforward recipes, this book is perfect for the sugar-free, grain-free newbie. Think going low-carb or Paleo means you will have to miss out on sweet treats and delicious baked goods? Dana and Caitlin turn that idea on its head. Enjoy everything from muffins and cookies to your favorite coffee house drinks, all without those pesky sugars and grains. They also include tips on grain-free baking and cooking, as well as how to source the necessary ingredients. Healthy living and clean eating start here.*"

—Carolyn Ketchum, Writer and Photographer
All Day I Dream About Food, alldayidreamaboutfood.com

"*I've been on a low-carb diet for three years, and rely totally on cookbooks like this to make it through. Dana and Caitlin's recipes really hit the sweet spot. Literally. Most recipes are low-carb, or have a low-carb option suitable for induction, but if you've adopted a Paleo lifestyle and don't need to do all that counting, there are variations for you. Plus, if you just want to get all that grain and sugar out of your life, and don't care about carbs or cavemen, then you're covered too. Best of all, for someone like me–not the most experienced cook in the kitchen–they encourage experimenting and learning, but at the same time keep you on the path toward great tasting dishes.*"

—Ed Stockly, TV Skeptic
Los Angeles Times, latimes.com/la-bio-ed-stockly-staff.html

CarbSmart Press

CarbSmart, Inc.
6165 Harrison Drive, Suite 1
Las Vegas, NV 89120

Dedication

As I approach the age of 50 this year, I am amazed that friends and relatives continue to ask if I still eat low-carb. I think it's the mindset that this lifestyle must be a (temporary) diet and I should probably be back on "regular" foods like whole grains, fruit, and anything low-fat by now.

But of course, the only reason I would stop eating a low-carb, ketogenic diet is if I wanted to become diabetic, morbidly obese, and unable to walk up and down stairs comfortably again. I'm sorry but that ain't happening.

This cookbook is dedicated to everyone who has successfully changed their life with a low-carb, ketogenic lifestyle. Whether you have lost a couple or couple hundred pounds; lowered your blood sugar and blood pressure levels, reduced your dependence on sugar, processed foods, and diabetes medication; know that you've improved your quality of life. So stand up, walk to a mirror and look at what you've accomplished. I am so proud of you.

Andrew S. DiMino
President, Publisher, and Founder
CarbSmart, Inc.

By *GlutenSmart Press*

Easy Gluten-Free Entertaining

by Christine Seelye-King & Aimee DuFresne

50 Delicious Gluten-Free Party Recipes For Every Occasion

A great book for anyone looking for entertainment ideas that just happen to be gluten-free.

Your next social gathering will be a success because the recipes included in <u>Easy Gluten-Free Entertaining</u> (carbsmart.com/go/gfsf-067.php) make it easy to satisfy any and all palates and preferences. From delicious appetizers to main dishes, side dishes, and dessert, look no further.

CONTENTS

Cookies 49

Cakes and Pies 61

CONTENTS

Acknowledgements 107

Resources 109

The Authors 115

Foreword

by Cassie Bjork

I used to be a sugar addict.

I'll never forget the time I ate an entire container of my roommate's frosted sugar cookies. I thought I'd sneak just one...or two. Before I knew it, the whole container was gone.

I'll never forget the feeling of shame and embarrassment when I had to confess what I'd done. Regret and shame lingered on with a feeling of helplessness. Not to mention the gut-wrenching indigestion. I didn't want to live like that. It didn't even feel like a choice. It was a compulsion of the worst kind, yet I didn't know what caused it. At the time, I was in school to become a dietitian and I was learning the importance of low-fat foods and whole grains. In retrospect, I know from personal experience that the low-fat, high carb way of eating was taking me for a ride on the blood sugar roller coaster all day long. I was never satisfied. I always needed more sugar. It was a vicious cycle that I have both experienced myself and seen others struggle with too.

The good news is that it is possible to get off that roller coaster, and it's really not that hard. If you've picked up this book, then you've likely already taken the first step. For me, that step was embracing healthy fats like butter, avocado, nuts, seeds and cream. The more fat I eat, the fewer carbs I crave. For others, it's ensuring they are consuming adequate protein during the day to keep them satisfied and support the production of neurotransmitters.

Now I can confidently say that I know how to stay in control of my sugar addiction. "Just don't eat it" was never the answer. Eating a PFC (protein, fat, carbohydrate) balanced diet was the answer.

PFC balanced is the approach that my team of health coaches uses to help our clients find freedom in food every single day.

It includes quality protein, healthy fat and nutrient dense carbs (PFC). I started Healthy Simple Life and Dietitian Cassie both to be companies that help people implement this health strategy into their lives—whether my team coaches them in person, via Skype or over the phone.

I know many people are struggling with sugar addiction and are desperate to overcome it. I've learned firsthand that no one wants to be deprived of things they think they need. But making the shift to real food is worthwhile, liberating and life-changing. It's just not always an easy process. To that end, I would have loved to have this cookbook full of grain-free, sugar-free recipes to ease my transition to a real food lifestyle.

For those considering a grain-free, sugar-free lifestyle, these recipes can help immensely. They are a far better choice than going back to processed, sugar-laden junk. I love that many of the recipes in here are also dairy-free. Many times when clients of ours find out they have a dairy sensitivity, it can be challenging to find ways to continue enjoying some of their favorite foods. Another common challenge is how to incorporate condiments without the added sugar. The ones in this cookbook are clean and free of the junk that's in most you'll find at the store. Protein can also be tricky to incorporate into snacks since a lot of the protein powders out there are loaded with sugar and artificial sweeteners. I recommend Ultimate Natural Whey Protein (carbsmart.com/go/gfsf-081.php) as it's pure whey protein and it's imported from New Zealand where rBGH is not approved for use.

While the treats and condiments in this cookbook are still just that—treats—you don't have to feel so guilty when you consume them. They are a much healthier alternative to picking up a junky cookie or milkshake from a fast food restaurant—something I used to do more often than I'd like to admit.

Now, although they're better than many options out there, I want to be clear about my stance on 2 things. First, when it comes to treats, I think it's important to recognize them for what they are—

by definition, they are not meant to be a regular part of a nutrition regimen. It's up to you to decide if they fit in as part of your balanced lifestyle.

Second, when it comes to sugar alcohols (like erythritol and xylitol), I'm not a big fan. Xylitol in particular can have some unpleasant side effects. Our bodies do a poor job digesting it, so it can hang out in our intestines where it is fermented by colonic bacteria. The by-products of fermentation can include gastric distress, diarrhea, cramping, gas and bloating. I'm more comfortable with using pure stevia or a little bit of real sugar. That said, I believe any recipe in this book is going to be a heck of a lot healthier than many other substitution recipes out there, and quality and type do matter. When using sugar alcohols and other sweeteners, it's smart to follow the particular guidelines outlined by Dana and Caitlin for choosing them, and then keep evaluating how they, along with treats in general, fit into your balanced lifestyle.

There are no better authors than Caitlin and Dana for this book, because they have both overcome health hurdles themselves with different, unique backgrounds, and they are both committed to helping others change their lives with whole, healing foods.

Start with real food. Include protein, fat and carbohydrates (PFC!). And add in the recipes in this book as you see fit on your journey to a real food lifestyle. Life is all about finding balance. Finding balance with your food, exercise, sleep, stress, family and yes, in some cases, balance even includes tasty treats and delicious condiments.

Cheers to real food,
Cassie Bjork, RD, LD
"Dietitian Cassie"
Owner and Lead Health Coach
Healthysimplelife.com
DietitianCassie.com

A Journey Towards Health and My Take on Sweet Treats

by Caitlin Weeks

I grew up in a southern family where food was the focal point of social activity. When I was 3 years old, I started to eat for comfort after my parents' divorce. I was a chubby adolescent and by the time I got out of college I was 240 pounds. I lost the weight on a low-fat diet then decided to become a personal trainer. I was basically an exercise-aholic for over 10 years and counted every calorie. After 5 years of training I decided that nutrition was my real passion so I became a holistic nutrition consultant. While I was in nutrition school I became very ill and rundown from the combination of a vegetarian diet and running marathons. I found out I had Hashimoto's Thyroiditis, which caused me to seek out therapeutic approaches for healing. I embraced low-carb, Paleo and Weston A. Price (carbsmart. com/go/gfsf-003.php) approaches during my long journey back to health. Now I write articles and recipes to educate and encourage other people on their journey to heal themselves with natural methods. You can find my articles at GrassFedGirl.com and CarbSmart.com (carbsmart.com/go/gfsf-008.php).

I am inspired to create these healthy recipes by my own journey back to health. I had to remove most inflammatory foods (gluten, soy, corn, dairy, sugar) for a period of time to calm down my autoimmune condition. During that process I found that there are many ways to create treats with wholesome ingredients that can fit into low-carb or Paleo plans. These treats can be enjoyed occasionally because they are gluten-free/grain-free, sugar-free, and free of manmade oils such as corn and soybean oil.

The less junk we eat the easier it will be to lose weight and stay away from the doctor's office. As a food blogger and nutritionist

I want to help people avoid the conventional wisdom that low-fat foods and calorie counting will make them healthy. I am inspired to create nutrient-dense recipes that will support people on a healing journey.

I worked with clients for many years and I saw them fall into the trap of eating processed diet food to try to lose weight, which never worked. I also saw them going to social events unprepared, only to end up bingeing on food that did not fit their goals. I want you, the readers of this book, to have options to make your eating plan sustainable. I have found that there can be some leeway on eating treats as long as they are made with wholesome ingredients that are full of nutrition but low in carbs.

A word about sugars and sweeteners: The two main sweeteners I have researched and experimented that I use in my recipes are stevia and xylitol.

Stevia

I usually use stevia at home when cooking or in drinks. Stevia is an ancient herb that has been used in Paraguay for centuries and in Japan for generations. It is a low-calorie, natural substance derived from the South American stevia plant. It does not affect blood sugar levels in my clients and, in my experience, it doesn't seem to be habit forming.

The main thing is to watch out for ingredients that are combined stevia. There are many additives combined with stevia to save money in processing and many of them are from genetically modified corn. Look for stevia from the dried green leaf if possible. The next best option is have a concentrated liquid or powder concentrate with no other ingredients. I use the stevia powder extract in these recipes, which is a concentrated form with no additives, meaning that very little is needed per recipe.

Xylitol

Xylitol (carbsmart.com/go/gfsf-045.php) is a sweetener that is extracted from the hardwoods of birch trees. It is also naturally found in low concentrations in the fibers of many fruits and vegetables. It has been studied for its benefits to teeth and gums. Make sure to choose organic birch xylitol, not one derived from corn. **Be aware that many people have a reaction to xylitol that is made from corn, which is usually genetically modified and heavily sprayed.**

Some people like xylitol more than stevia because it is granulated, making it easier to work with. It's usually a 1-to-1 exchange with sugar in recipes even though it is not quite as sweet as sugar. Unlike stevia, xylitol does not have an aftertaste but it can have a laxative effect if used in excess. It is not something to have on a daily basis, but can be a good sugar substitute for occasional indulgences. These recipes will fit in to a Paleo and low-carb, gluten-free diet very nicely.

As a nutritionist I urge you to have well-rounded meals full of grass fed proteins, natural fats and organic veggies for the main part of your diet. I wanted to write this book as resource for healthy options when someone feels the need for a sweet treat that won't derail their healthy, real food lifestyle. I hope you will choose these recipes when looking for something to satisfy a sweet craving rather than buying junk at the store.

In health -
Caitlin Weeks
GrassFedGirl.com

Ingredients for Grain-Free, Sugar-Free Living

by Dana Carpender

Welcome! There are all kinds of reasons you may be shunning grains, sugar, or both: You may be a low carber, like I've been since 1995. You may be eating a Paleo diet, like Caitlin. You may have Celiac Disease or some other grain sensitivity. You may be diabetic or pre-diabetic. Or you may, like some of us, have simply decided that neither grains nor sugar are wholesome and that they are not really food for human beings.

Whatever your reason, we hope this book will serve you well, not only supplying recipes you'll use over and over, but giving you a primer on the subject of grain- and sugar-free cooking, so you can go on and create your own recipes.

As for the whole question of organic-versus-conventionally grown, grocery store dairy products versus grass-fed or even grass-fed and raw, that sort of thing, we leave it up to you. Caitlin eats 'cleaner' than I do. I keep an eye on the Environmental Working Group (carbsmart.com/go/gfsf-009.php) Dirty Dozen and Clean Fifteen lists–the lists of which produce is mostly likely to be pesticide-laden versus which is likely to be pretty clean, even in its conventionally grown (and cheaper) forms. I buy both grass-fed and conventional dairy, depending on the budget that week. Since I have chickens in the back yard, I eat local pastured eggs (can't get 'em any more local than that), and I will spring for pastured eggs at the health food store when my chickens aren't laying. I eat a lot of eggs.

You'll definitely want to find a good health food store, preferably one that carries nuts, seeds, teas, herbs, and the like in bulk–they're much cheaper that way. But thanks to the internet, anything you can't buy locally you can easily order–Amazon.com (carbsmart.com/go/gfsf-001.php) carries an astonishing array of specialty groceries, as does Netrition.com (carbsmart.com/go/gfsf-005. php). I love Mountain Rose Herbs (carbsmart.com/go/gfsf-006.php) for bulk herbs, and Penzeys Spices (carbsmart.com/go/gfsf-007.php) has a marvelous reputation for spices. Our own sister website, NevadaManna.com, carries a wide selection of ingredients that are grain-free and sugar-free.

Speaking of specialty products, let's talk about sweeteners. Artificial sweeteners are definitely not Paleo, and many low carbers have moved away from them. To keep this book useful for the widest possible audience, we haven't used them. Instead, you'll find a few more natural* sweeteners used repeatedly.

* About that word "natural"–I have to repeat here what I have said many times before, that the idea that "natural" means "harmless" is specious. Rattlesnake venom is natural, but hardly harmless. That's not to say that I consider the sweeteners in this book dangerous. I don't; though I do think that moderation even with sugar-free sweetened products is merited. I just grit my teeth when I hear the word "natural" used as a synonym for "safe."

We have created an entire resource section as easy-to-use lists.

Grain-Free, Sugar-Free ingredients list at CarbSmart.com:
carbsmart.com/go/gfsf-085.php

Grain-Free, Sugar-Free ingredients list at Amazon.com:
carbsmart.com/go/gfsf-001.php

Grain-Free, Sugar-Free ingredients list at NevadaManna.com:
carbsmart.com/go/gfsf-080.php

Stevia

Stevia, as most people know by now, is a South American herb with extremely sweet leaves. There are several forms available. In this book, my recipes call for liquid stevia extract (carbsmart.com/go/gfsf-011.php), both plain–i.e. just sweet–and flavored. I've used vanilla (carbsmart.com/go/gfsf-012.php), chocolate (carbsmart.com/go/gfsf-013.php), English toffee (carbsmart.com/go/gfsf-014.php), and even lemon drop (carbsmart.com/go/gfsf-015.php) flavored stevia.

It's important to know the sweetness equivalence of your stevia–how much to equal 1 teaspoon of sugar in sweetness. My recipes use liquid stevia that has a sweetness equivalence to sugar of 6 drops stevia extract = 1 teaspoon sugar, I use SweetLeaf (carbsmart.com/go/gfsf-016.php), NOW (carbsmart.com/go/gfsf-017.php), and NuNaturals (carbsmart.com/go/gfsf-018.php) brands. EZ-Sweetz (carbsmart.com/go/gfsf-019.php), known among low carbers for their liquid sucralose (carbsmart.com/go/gfsf-020.php), makes liquid stevia (carbsmart.com/go/gfsf-021.php) and a liquid stevia/monk fruit blend (carbsmart.com/go/gfsf-022.php), as well. These are considerably sweeter than some other stevia products–2 drops = 1 teaspoon sugar in sweetness, so you'll have to do some elementary arithmetic to adjust quantities.

Some of these recipes call for dried stevia leaf–this is particularly useful for sweetening tea, since you can just add it with whatever other herbs you're using.

Both liquid stevia extracts and dried stevia leaf are available at health food stores, or, like everything else in the world, online at Amazon.com. I buy dried stevia in bulk from Mountain Rose herbs.

Erythritol

Erythritol (carbsmart.com/go/gfsf-024.php) is a member of the sugar alcohol or polyol class of sweeteners–carbohydrates with a molecule that is large and hard for the human body to digest and absorb. I like erythritol for a couple of reasons: First of all, because it passes through the body unchanged, erythritol has no effect on blood sugar or insulin at all. Secondly, unlike most of the sugar alcohols, erythritol causes virtually no gas or gastric disturbance.

There are a few challenges to using erythritol. It's not quite as sweet as sugar, so it takes a little experimentation to work out equivalencies to sugar. It is endothermic–when it hits the moisture in your mouth it literally absorbs energy, creating a cooling effect. This is fine in ice cream, but a little odd in brownies. And it crystallizes readily, sometimes causing a gritty result. Plus erythritol is not cheap–generally between $7-10/lb.

For all of these reasons, I often combine erythritol with stevia (carbsmart.com/go/gfsf-025.php). Erythritol is available in both granular and powdered form; both are quite useful. If you can't find powdered erythritol, running the granular stuff through the food processor for a few minutes will yield a reasonably good simulacrum.

Swerve

Swerve is my go-to sweetener for baking purposes. It is mostly erythritol, but has some fructooligosaccharides–sweet-tasting fiber–added to increase the sweetness and make it behave more like sugar. In particular, it caramelizes–browns–more than erythritol.

Swerve has the cooling effect of erythritol. It is also even more expensive than straight erythritol, usually $9-12/lb. I find it worth the price, and keep both granular (carbsmart.com/go/gfsf-026.php) and confectioner's style (powdered) (carbsmart.com/go/gfsf-027.php) Swerve in the house. I have specified it in many of these recipes, but plain erythritol should do fine.

Xylitol

Caitlin prefers xylitol (carbsmart.com/go/gfsf-028.php). Originally derived from birch trees, xylitol is another of the sugar alcohols. It has the unique property of being protective of teeth–eating a bit of xylitol every day can actually improve your oral health.

Unlike erythritol, some of xylitol is digested and absorbed, but it's easier on blood sugar than table sugar. However, if you eat too much of it you are likely to become, uh, socially offensive. At larger doses–what constitutes "larger doses" is an individual thing–it acts as a laxative. So go easy.

Be aware that xylitol is profoundly toxic to dogs. If you share your home with pooches, be extremely careful with xylitol-sweetened foods. One cookie could kill your best friend. (This is why I don't use xylitol–I have three dogs, and just can't risk it.)

Yacon Syrup

I've used this in just a few recipes to get a flavor similar to brown sugar or molasses. Yacon, an Andean root, has been a traditional South American food for centuries. Due to a large percentage of fructooligosaccharides–sweet fiber–yacon syrup has a low blood sugar impact, and there are preliminary studies suggesting that it decreases weight and waist circumference. However, it does contain fructose, so I still won't be chugging it down. In the quantities I've used it here I consider it harmless. I had to order yacon syrup (carbsmart.com/go/gfsf-029.php) online; none of my local health food stores carry it yet, and it's not cheap. Depending on how "clean" you want to eat, you could substitute molasses. In the quantities used here, it's unlikely to do you harm.

Other Ingredients Worth Mentioning:

Almond Meal

The widely distributed Bob's Red Mill (carbsmart.com/go/gfsf-031.php) brand has a good one, and it's often found in the baking aisle of regular grocery stores. NOW foods has one as well, mostly distributed through health food stores. If you really want to, you can just run shelled almonds through your food processor until they reach the texture of cornmeal.

Coconut Flour

Bob's Red Mill (carbsmart.com/go/gfsf-032.php) is the brand I use. Do not confuse coconut flour for shredded or ground coconut. It is made from the residue left after coconut oil is pressed out of the meat. It has a tremendous quantity of fiber–and something of a learning curve. Coconut flour may or may not be in the baking aisle of your grocery store, but should be at your health food store.

Flaxseed Meal

Once again, Bob's Red Mill (carbsmart.com/go/gfsf-033.php) is my favorite. They package a golden flax seed meal that is excellent, and is frequently available in grocery stores.

Chia Seed

Rapidly growing in popularity, chia is not just for growing "hair" on terra cotta statuettes anymore. It's highly nutritious. It is also loaded with soluble fiber, giving it considerable thickening properties so it can be used similarly to xanthan gum or guar gum to give structure to gluten-free baked goods. I buy chia seed (carbsmart.com/go/gfsf-030.php) in bulk at my health food store.

Vanilla Whey

I like to combine vanilla whey protein powder with nut meal for baking purposes—it tastes great and yields a good texture. I've used several brands of vanilla whey protein over the years, and all of them have worked fine. Designer Whey (carbsmart.com/go/gfsf-034.php) is probably the most widely available; GNC stores carry it. Recently I've been using Vitacost.com's house brand (carbsmart.com/go/gfsf-035.php) because it's inexpensive, and I find it excellent.

Coconut

I use quite a lot of coconut, both shredded (carbsmart.com/go/gfsf-036.php) and flaked (carbsmart.com/go/gfsf-037.php). It's worth your while to find a health food store that carries these in the bulk bins; you'll save considerable money. Look for a store with brisk turnover to get the freshest product.

Sunflower Seeds

I love sunflower seeds (carbsmart.com/go/gfsf-038.php) for crackers and crusts. These recipes call for hulled, raw sunflower seeds. If you buy the roasted, salted ones, your recipes won't come out right. Again, a good health food store should have raw, hulled sunflower seeds in bulk.

MCT Oil

I've only mentioned this once or twice. MCT oil (carbsmart.com/go/gfsf-039.php), or medium-chain triglyceride oil, is derived from coconut oil, but unlike coconut oil it is liquid at room temperature. Medium-chain triglycerides are highly ketogenic saturated fats that can be used directly for fuel by your muscles. I like to use it when I want a bland oil.

How to Use This Cookbook

Welcome to the **Grain-Free, Sugar-Free Living Cookbook** by Dana Carpender and Caitlin Weeks, NC! Just a few notes about the book before you dig in. In the authors' introductions, you will find lists of the most healthful sweeteners and other ingredients common to our recipes. These lists include what the ingredient is derived from and how best to use it.

We've tried to make the process of adapting the recipes to your individual needs simple. You may notice that the authors use different sweeteners. This is because their approach to food is different. Dana is a long-term advocate and follower of low-carb, while Caitlin is a Paleo nutrition specialist. Paleo recipes also tend to be a bit higher in carbs and a little more forgiving with natural sweeteners. To that end, you will notice that there is a tag line below the author's name on each recipe. The tags designate the categories into which the recipe fits a specific dietary need.

Stevia will not take the place of sugar or sugar alcohols in baking without changing the texture. You may want to consider substituting a combination of xylitol or erythtitol with the stevia. Erythritol and xylitol generally do not change the texture of traditional baked goods too much. If your preference is to eliminate erythritol and xylitol altogether, we suggest experimenting with the other ingredients in the recipes a bit in order to achieve the desired texture.

Please note: The following sweetener conversion chart does not account for texture differentials.

Sweetener - based on sugar equivalent	1 Cup	1 Tablespoon	1 Teaspoon
Xylitol	1 Cup	1 Tablespoon	1 Teaspoon
Erythritol	1 Cup	1 Tablespoon	1 Teaspoon
Splenda	1 Cup	1 Tablespoon	1 Teaspoon
Swerve	1 Cup	1 Tablespoon	1 Teaspoon
Stevia —Whole Leaf Powder	2 Tablespoons	$\frac{3}{8}$ Tablespoon	$\frac{1}{8}$ Teaspoon
Stevia —Spoonable Powder	2¼ Tablespoons	½ Teaspoon	$\frac{1}{6}$ Teaspoon
Stevia —Liquid	48 Drops	3 Drops	1 Drop
Stevia —Flavored Liquid	48-50 Drops	3-5 Drops	1-2 Drops
Honey	½ Cup	½ Tablespoon	½ Teaspoon
Maple Syrup	½ Cup	½ Tablespoon	½ Teaspoon
Coconut Sugar	1 Cup	1 Tablespoon	1 Teaspoon

Low-Carb

The term refers to an eating plan that advises limiting the consumption of high carbohydrate foods. Also referred to as low glycemic and ketogenic, a low-carb diet seeks to balance metabolic processes and prevent chronic illness such as diabetes.

Gluten-Free

A diet that excludes the protein gluten found in such grains as wheat, barley, rye, and triticale. A gluten-free diet is used to treat Celiac disease and other gluten intolerant illnesses by preventing inflammation in the small intestine.

Paleo

Although there are many variations of the Paleo Diet, at their core, they all consist of whole, unprocessed, nutrient dense foods such as fish, grass-fed pasture-raised meats, eggs, vegetables, fruit, tubers, and nuts. Most Paleo diets omit grains, legumes, dairy products, and refined salts and sugars. Paleo is an all-natural low-carb diet that is slightly higher in carbohydrates than plans such as Atkins, Protein Power, or Zone.

Paleo (optional)

Refers to recipes which are low-carb but not necessarily Paleo but can easily be converted to Paleo. These recipes will offer alternative ingredients in their listing to make the conversion to Paleo seamless.

Vegetarian

These recipes do not contain meat or fish but may contain dairy, eggs, and honey.

Vegan

Refers to recipes that contain no animal or animal by-products. They are free of dairy, eggs, and honey.

Dairy-Free

Contain no dairy products.

Nut-Free

Contain no nuts or nut products.

Toward the end of the book, you will find Resource Lists that contain everything from our favorite retailers to equipment and tools to make your cooking experience fun and easy.

We hope you enjoy the recipes in this book and that they bring you and your family many happy food dances!

From our table to yours, Happy Eating!

Condiments

Condiments are notoriously packed with sugar, grains, and of course preservatives. It's time to ditch the store bought stuff in favor of these fresh, healthy, and delicious homemade alternatives. All the taste without the guilt and we promise it won't take much time to prepare!

Dana's Stevia-Sweetened Ketchup

by Dana Carpender

Low-Carb, Gluten-Free, Paleo (optional), Vegetarian, Dairy-Free, Nut-Free

Everybody's favorite condiment is simply loaded with sugar. I've made my own for years. I've published Splenda-sweetened recipes, but here's one with Swerve and stevia.

Prep time: 5 minutes

Cooking time: 30 minutes

Yield: 1½ cups

INGREDIENTS

8 ounces organic plain canned tomato sauce

⅔ cup apple cider vinegar

¼ cup powdered Swerve (carbsmart.com/go/gfsf-027.php)

¼ teaspoon liquid stevia extract (carbsmart.com/go/gfsf-078.php)

2 tablespoons minced onion

2 garlic cloves

⅛ teaspoon ground allspice

⅛ teaspoon ground cloves

⅛ teaspoon ground pepper

salt to taste

PREPARATION AND INSTRUCTIONS

Put everything but the salt in your food processor or blender, and run until the onion and garlic are pulverized.

Pour into a small non-reactive saucepan. Bring to a bare simmer, and let it cook for 20-30 minutes. Taste, then add salt. ½-1 teaspoon should be about right. You can add a few extra drops of stevia extract if you think it needs it, as well.

Store in a snap-top container in the fridge, and use for all ketchup-y purposes.

NUTRITIONAL INFO

12 servings of 2 tablespoons, each with: 9 Calories; trace Fat (3.3% calories from fat); trace Protein; 2g Carbohydrate; trace Dietary Fiber; 2g Usable Carbs.

Amazing Steak Sauce

by Dana Carpender

Low-Carb, Gluten-Free, Paleo (optional), Dairy-Free, Nut-Free

That Nice Boy I Married and I tested this by using it to top a grass-fed hamburger, along with some caramelized onions. Amazing!

Prep time: 5 minutes

Cooking time: 15 minutes

Yield: 1½ cups

¼ teaspoon liquid stevia extract (carbsmart.com/go/gfsf-011.php)

INGREDIENTS

¼ cup white balsamic vinegar

¼ cup red wine vinegar

¼ cup lemon juice

2 tablespoons zante currants or about 2½ tablespoons raisins

¼ cup San-J gluten-free soy sauce (carbsmart.com/go/gfsf-040.php)–If you're avoiding soy altogether you can substitute coconut aminos (carbsmart.com/go/gfsf-041.php).

¼ teaspoon gluten-free xanthan gum

2 tablespoons spicy brown mustard or Dijon mustard

½ teaspoon orange extract

¼ cup Dana's Stevia Sweetened Ketchup (page 34)

1 tablespoon yacon syrup (carbsmart.com/go/gfsf-029.php)

¼ teaspoon chili powder

1 teaspoon anchovy paste

2 tablespoons Swerve Granular (carbsmart.com/go/gfsf-026.php)

PREPARATION AND INSTRUCTIONS

In a small, non-reactive saucepan, combine the white balsamic vinegar, red wine vinegar, lemon juice, currants, and soy sauce. Bring to a simmer and cook for 10-15 minutes.

Pour mixture into your blender, add the xanthan gum, and run until the currants are pulverized. Blend in everything else. Pour back into the saucepan.

Bring back to a simmer, and cook gently for another 10-15 minutes. I like to store this in a squeeze bottle; it's easy to use that way.

NOTES

If you cook this in a larger saucepan than I did, it will cook down faster. Keep an eye on it!

NUTRITIONAL INFO

12 servings of 2 tablespoons, each with:
16 Calories; trace Fat (13.8% calories from fat); 1g Protein; 3g Carbohydrate; trace Dietary Fiber; 3g Usable Carbs.

Eric's Barbecue Sauce

by Dana Carpender

Low-Carb, Gluten-Free, Paleo (optional), Dairy-Free, Nut-Free

Eric is also known as That Nice Boy I Married, and he grew up just outside Kansas City, so this is a KC-style barbecue sauce. Guaranteed to tickle your taste buds.

Prep time: 5 minutes

Cooking time: 15 minutes

Yield: 2 Cups

INGREDIENTS

1 clove garlic, crushed

¼ cup minced onion

2 tablespoons coconut oil–bland, not extra virgin

1 tablespoon lemon juice

1 batch Dana's Stevia Sweetened Ketchup (page 34)

1 tablespoon yacon syrup

1 tablespoon San-J gluten-free soy sauce or coconut aminos

½ teaspoon anchovy paste

1 tablespoon chili powder

1 tablespoon cider vinegar

1 teaspoon pepper

1 tablespoon liquid smoke flavoring (carbsmart.com/go/gfsf-042.php) (optional–read the labels to find a sugar-free, gluten-free version)

salt to taste

PREPARATION AND INSTRUCTIONS

In a non-reactive saucepan, over low heat, sauté garlic and onion in the coconut oil until they are soft.

Add everything else except the salt and stir it all up. Bring to a simmer, and let it cook for 10 minutes or so.

Salt to taste. Store in a snap-top container in the fridge, and use like any barbecue sauce.

NUTRITIONAL INFO

16 servings of 2 tablespoons, each with: 26 Calories; 2g Fat (56.7% calories from fat); trace Protein; 3g Carbohydrate; trace Dietary Fiber; 3g Usable Carbs.

Odd Predilections Dressing

by Dana Carpender

Low-Carb, Gluten-Free, Paleo, Vegetarian, Dairy-Free, Nut-Free

For those of you who enjoy the "foul beast," Miracle Whip, here's a sweet-and-tangy dressing with no sugar. I grew up in a mayonnaise household, but I ran this by a friend who grew up in a Miracle Whip household. She said this was similar, but better.

Prep time: 5-10 minutes

Cooking time: None

Yield: 1 Cup or 16 servings

INGREDIENTS

1 egg yolk

2 tablespoons white vinegar

24 drops liquid stevia extract–or to equal 4 teaspoons sugar in sweetness

¼ teaspoon salt, rounded

1½ teaspoons lemon juice

½ teaspoon dry mustard

1 pinch paprika

⅓ garlic clove, crushed, or a pinch of garlic powder

1 cup light olive oil or MCT oil (carbsmart.com/go/gfsf-039.php), or a combination of both

PREPARATION AND INSTRUCTIONS

Put everything but the oil in your food processor or blender, and run for 30 seconds or so. While that's happening, measure your oil in a measuring cup with a pouring lip.

With the processor or blender running, pour in the oil in a stream about the diameter of a pencil lead; don't pour too fast. When all the oil is added, turn off the machine. You're done! Store in a snap top container in the fridge.

NUTRITIONAL INFO

16 servings of 1 tablespoon, each with: 124 Calories; 14g Fat (98.7% calories from fat); trace Protein; trace Carbohydrate; trace Dietary Fiber; 0g Usable Carb.

"Honey" Mustard Dip

by Dana Carpender

Low-Carb, Gluten-Free, Paleo (optional), Vegetarian, Dairy-Free, Nut-Free

This yummy dip is great for snacking with fresh veggies, chicken, or shrimp. It's super quick and easy to make and it keeps well in the fridge, if you need to prepare ahead of time for a party.

Prep time: 5 minutes

Cooking time: None

Yield: 1½ cups

INGREDIENTS

1½ cups mayonnaise (homemade is way better for you than store-bought) or Odd Predilections Dressing (page 37)

2 tablespoons brown mustard

¼ teaspoon liquid stevia extract

½ teaspoon Creole seasoning (carbsmart.com/go/gfsf-043.php)–or up to 1½ teaspoons

PREPARATION AND INSTRUCTIONS

Simple! Just stir everything up, and use as a dip for vegetables, chicken, shrimp–anything you like to dip in honey mustard sauce.

NUTRITIONAL INFO

24 servings of 1 tablespoon, each with: 100 Calories; 12g Fat (98.6% calories from fat); trace Protein; trace Carbohydrate; trace Dietary Fiber; 0g Usable Carb.

Stevia Bread and Butter Pickles

by Dana Carpender

Low-Carb, Gluten-Free, Paleo (optional), Vegetarian, Dairy-Free, Nut-Free

Sugar-free sweet pickles are available in many grocery stores, but invariably they have artificial sweeteners. These don't, and they taste better, too!

Prep time: 5 minutes

Cooking time: 10 minutes

INGREDIENTS

32 ounces organic pickles (Plain sour pickles, no dill.)

1 teaspoon liquid stevia extract

½ teaspoon allspice
(or better, a few whole allspice berries)

½ teaspoon celery seed

1½ teaspoons mustard seed

1 pinch ground cloves

PREPARATION AND INSTRUCTIONS

Drain the liquid from your jar of pickles into a non-reactive saucepan.

Add everything else, and bring to a simmer.

Let it cook a few minutes to let the flavors blend, then let it cool just a minute or two before pouring the seasoned brine back into the jar.

Put the lid on and stash in the fridge. Let 'em marinate for at least a few days before using, then use like any sweet pickles.

NOTES

Bonus! If you need sweet pickle relish, chopping this up a bit in your food processor will make a great substitute.

NUTRITIONAL INFO

This whole batch will have: 197 Calories; 4g Fat (14.3% calories from fat); 7g Protein; 40g Carbohydrate; 12g Dietary Fiber; 28g Usable Carbs. Carbs per serving will depend on whether you're using pickle chips, spears, whatever.

Beverages

We offer you a collection of recipes for a variety of delicious hot and cold beverages including smoothies, flavored coffees, and teas. Whether you're searching for the perfect party beverage or an afternoon treat for two, you will find our sugar free drinks delectable.

Paleo Peanut Butter Cup Smoothie

by Caitlin Weeks

Low-Carb (optional), Gluten-Free, Paleo, Dairy-Free, Contains Nuts

One of my long time readers asked for this smoothie so I tried to make it taste as good as my memories. This only has one banana so if you split it with a friend it won't have too many carbs. You can also substitute frozen strawberries or other berries if you want fewer carbs. The gelatin adds protein so the smoothie will stick with you longer.

Prep time: 5 minutes

Cooking time: N/A

INGREDIENTS

1 tray ice cubes (about 12 cubes)

½ cup frozen strawberries for low-carb version or 1 frozen banana for Paleo version

¼ cup almond butter or sugar-free peanut butter for non-Paleo version

1 cup full fat coconut milk (carbsmart.com/go/gfsf-053.php), canned

2 tablespoons cocoa powder

¼ cup birch xylitol (carbsmart.com/go/gfsf-045.php) or 1 teaspoon stevia powder extract (carbsmart.com/go/gfsf-046.php)

½ teaspoon sea salt

2 tablespoons gelatin (Great Lakes Gelatin, Collagen Hydrolysate carbsmart.com/go/gfsf-044.php is what I use)

PREPARATION AND INSTRUCTIONS

Mix all the ingredients in the blender except for the gelatin.

Once the ingredients are blended, add the gelatin and blend a few more seconds.

Pour into two glasses and serve with a straw.

VARIATIONS

Replace frozen banana with frozen strawberries, blueberries, or raspberries if you want fewer carbs but still a great taste.

NUTRITIONAL INFO WITH STRAWBERRIES

Serves 2; Per Serving: 520 Calories; 47g Fat (417 calories from fat); 0mg Cholesterol; 496 mg Sodium; 14.7g Protein; 10.2g Carbohydrate; 4.6g Dietary Fiber; 5.6g Usable Carbs.

NUTRITIONAL INFO WITH BANANA

Serves 2; Per Serving: 585 Calories; 47g Fat (423 calories from fat); 0mg Cholesterol; 501mg Sodium; 16.8g Protein; 34.6g Carbohydrate; 7.4g Dietary Fiber; 27.2g Usable Carbs.

Vanilla Toffee Coffee

by Dana Carpender

Low-Carb, Gluten-Free, Paleo (optional)

You know that those sweetened coffee drinks are full of sugar, right? Here is a quick and easy alternative to those overpriced, sugar laden coffee house drinks.

Prep time: 5 minutes

Cooking time: N/A

Serves: 2

INGREDIENTS

½ cup heavy cream, chilled or Coconut Milk Whipped Cream (page 90)

12 drops English toffee flavor liquid stevia extract (carbsmart.com/go/gfsf-014.php)

8 drops French Vanilla flavor liquid stevia extract (carbsmart.com/go/gfsf-012.php)

12 fluid ounces brewed coffee

PREPARATION AND INSTRUCTIONS

If using heavy cream, whip with the two stevia extracts until stiff.

Divide coffee into two mugs, and top with the sweetened whipped cream or Coconut Milk Whipped Cream (page 90). Luscious!

NUTRITIONAL INFO

Per Serving: 209 Calories; 22g Fat (93.0% calories from fat); 1g Protein; 2g Carbohydrate; 0g Dietary Fiber; 2g Usable Carbs.

Dairy-Free Frozen Mochaccino

by Caitlin Weeks

Low-Carb, Gluten-Free, Paleo, Vegetarian, Dairy-Free, Contains Nuts

I love Starbucks as much as the next person, but their drinks are so full of sugar and chemicals. I wanted to make a drink at home that would fit into a lower carb lifestyle with natural ingredients. Top it with the Coconut Milk Whipped Cream (page 90) for a sweet finish.

Prep time: 5 minutes

Cooking time: N/A

Serves: 1

INGREDIENTS

¾ cup double-strength coffee

½ teaspoon stevia powder extract

½ cup almond milk

3 tablespoons cocoa powder

2 cups ice cubes

PREPARATION AND INSTRUCTIONS

Combine all ingredients in the blender until smooth, about 30 seconds.

Pour in a cup and drink with a straw

Top with Coconut Milk Whipped Cream (page 90) if desired.

NUTRITIONAL INFO

Serves 1; Per Serving: 60 Calories; 3.6g Fat (33 calories from fat); 0mg Cholesterol; 111mg Sodium; 3.7g Protein; 9.9g Carbohydrate; 5.3g Dietary Fiber; 4.6g Usable Carbs.

Lemonade By The Glass

by Dana Carpender

Low-Carb, Gluten-Free, Paleo, Vegetarian, Dairy-Free, Nut-Free

This is also great made with chilled sparkling water–plain, lemon, lime, or my favorite, berry. It is refreshing and satisfying and the whole family will love it!

Prep time: 3 minutes

Cooking time: N/A

Serves: 1

INGREDIENTS

3 tablespoons lemon juice

18 drops lemon flavor liquid stevia extract (carbsmart.com/go/gfsf-015.php)

Ice

Water

PREPARATION AND INSTRUCTIONS

Fill a tall glass with ice.

Add the lemon juice and lemon stevia extract.

Then add water to fill.

NUTRITIONAL INFO

1 serving with: 11 Calories; 0g Fat (0.0% calories from fat); trace Protein; 4g Carbohydrate; trace Dietary Fiber; 4g Usable Carbs

Hibiscus Tea

by Dana Carpender

Low-Carb, Gluten-Free, Paleo, Vegetarian, Dairy-Free

So very simple, delicious, and nutritious, this beautiful red tea tastes a lot like a fruit punch, but without the carbs. Loaded with antioxidants, too!

Prep time: 5 minutes
Cooking time: 1 hour
Yield: ½ gallon   Serves: 8

INGREDIENTS

1 cup dried hibiscus flowers

3 tablespoons <u>dried stevia leaf</u> (carbsmart.com/go/gfsf-023.php) (I like it like this, but if you want more or less, who am I to argue?)

2 cups boiling water

6 cups cold water

PREPARATION AND INSTRUCTIONS

Put both herbs in a ½ gallon pitcher. Pour the boiling water over them, and allow them to steep until they cool.

Now strain out the hibiscus and stevia leaf, pressing hard to get all the liquid out. Pour this tea concentrate back into the pitcher.

Add the cold water and stir. Keep chilled in the fridge for a refreshing beverage any time!

NUTRITIONAL INFO

8 servings, each with: 3 Calories; trace Fat (1.6% calories from fat); trace Protein; 1g Carbohydrate, trace fiber. However, you won't get that 1 gram of Usable Carb, since some of that carb content is strained out with the flowers and stevia leaves. I'd count about 0.5g per glass.

NOTES

This is wonderful over ice as-is, but try it mixed half-and-half with chilled berry sparkling water, too.

"Better Than Coffee Shop" Mocha

by Dana Carpender

Low-Carb, Gluten-Free, Paleo (optional), Vegetarian

This is not seriously low-carb, but it sure is lower carb than most coffee shop drinks. Some do have sugar-free syrups, but if you're also avoiding artificial sweeteners, those won't do. This will! Feel free to make this a cup at a time using 6 ounces of half and half, 6 ounces of coffee, about 18-20 drops of chocolate stevia extract, and a teaspoon of cocoa powder. You'll just have leftover whipped cream. Which means you'll need to keep it in the fridge, ready to make another cup. Shucky-darn.

Prep time: 5 minutes

Cooking time: 5 minutes

Serves: 3

INGREDIENTS

½ cup heavy cream, chilled or full fat coconut milk, chilled

12 drops French Vanilla liquid stevia extract

18 fluid ounces half and half or almond milk

18 fluid ounces brewed coffee

¼ teaspoon chocolate flavored liquid stevia extract (carbsmart.com/go/gfsf-013.php)

1 tablespoon cocoa powder

PREPARATION AND INSTRUCTIONS

First you need to whip your cream. If using coconut milk, be sure to separate the cream from the water. Then pour it into a small, deep mixing bowl, add the vanilla stevia, and use your electric mixer (NOT a hand blender!) or a whisk to whip it until it's nearly stiff. Don't overbeat, or you'll get vanilla butter!

You need to heat your half-and-half or almond milk; you want it as hot as your fresh-brewed coffee. You can do this in a saucepan on the stove, or in the microwave, just get it nice and hot.

While the half and half or almond milk is heating and the coffee is brewing, measure the stevia extract and cocoa powder into your blender.

Pour in both the coffee and half-and-half or almond milk, and run the blender for a minute or two until frothy.

Pour into three cups, divide the whipped cream between them, and drink!

NUTRITIONAL INFO

3 servings, each with: 381 Calories; 36g Fat (82.3% calories from fat); 7g Protein; 11g Carbohydrate; 1g Dietary Fiber; 10g Usable Carbs.

NOTES

If you like, make this with English Toffee flavored liquid stevia instead, leaving out the cocoa powder.

Cookies

Is there anything more enticing than the smell of fresh baked cookies right out of the oven? Cookies are the world's great comfort food. Here you will find the treats of your childhood memories as well as cookies for the more sophisticated pallet; an irresistible assortment of cookies that are all sugar-free and grain-free!

Super-Magic Cookie Bars

by Dana Carpender

Low-Carb, Gluten-Free, Paleo (optional), Vegetarian, Contains Nuts

You think the original was magical? Hah! I pulled off the same trick without grain or sugar.

Prep time: 15 minutes

Cooking time: 1 hour

Serves: 24

4 egg yolks

½ teaspoon English toffee flavor liquid stevia extract

INGREDIENTS

1 stick butter or 4 ounces extra virgin coconut oil
(carbsmart.com/go/gfsf-050.php)

¾ cup flax seed meal
(carbsmart.com/go/gfsf-033.php)

¾ cup almond meal
(carbsmart.com/go/gfsf-031.php)

½ teaspoon salt

¾ cup powdered Swerve
separated into ¼ cup and ½ cup

¼ cup vanilla whey protein powder
(carbsmart.com/go/gfsf-074.php)

1 cup sugar-free chocolate chips
(carbsmart.com/go/gfsf-047.php) or
Equal Exchange Organic Semi-Sweet
Chocolate Chips
(carbsmart.com/go/gfsf-075.php)(these
chocolate chips contain sugar which is safe
for Paleo but not low-carb)

1½ cups flaked unsweetened coconut meat
(carbsmart.com/go/gfsf-037.php)

1 cup chopped pecans or walnuts

¾ cup heavy cream or full fat coconut milk

¾ cup half and half or almond milk

PREPARATION AND INSTRUCTIONS

Preheat oven to 325° F. Line a 9" x 13" baking pan with non-stick foil.

While the oven's warming, throw the butter in the pan and stick it in the oven to melt. In the meanwhile...

Stir together the flax seed meal, almond meal, salt, ¼ cup Swerve, and the vanilla whey.

When the butter is melted, tilt the pan to spread it out over the bottom of the pan, then sprinkle the flax/almond mixture over it. Stir the whole thing gently, taking care not to rip the foil, until the crumbs are equally mixed with the butter. Pat into an even layer in the bottom of the pan.

Sprinkle the sugar-free chocolate chips, flaked unsweetened coconut meat, and chopped pecans or walnuts evenly over the almond/flax layer, in the order given.

Now whisk together everything else–I did this in my 2 cup Pyrex measure. Pour evenly over the whole thing.

Put the pan in the oven and set the timer for 1 hour.

When time's up, take a look–you want your bars equally set and golden brown all the way across. If they're still lighter colored and pretty soft in the middle, turn the oven down to 300° F and give them another 15-20 minutes.

When done, pull the pan out of the oven and let the whole thing cool before cutting into bars.

NUTRITIONAL INFO

24 bars, each with: 244 Calories; 20g Fat (71.0% calories from fat); 7g Protein; 11g Carbohydrate; 8g Dietary Fiber; 3g Usable Carbs.

Dana's Scrumptious Chocolate Chip Cookies

by Dana Carpender

Low-Carb, Gluten-Free, Paleo (optional), Vegetarian, Contains Nuts

The ideal chocolate chip cookie is crisp at the edges, and soft and gooey in the middle. This is my idea of cookie nirvana!

Prep time: 10 minutes

Cooking time: 10-12 minutes

Yields: 44 Cookies

INGREDIENTS

1 cup almond meal

1 cup vanilla whey protein powder

1 teaspoon baking soda

½ teaspoon corn-free baking powder (carbsmart.com/go/gfsf-076.php)

½ teaspoon salt

1 cup (2 sticks) butter, softened or 1 cup extra virgin coconut oil

¾ cup granular Swerve

½ teaspoon English Toffee flavor liquid stevia extract

1 tablespoon yacon syrup

2 eggs

3 teaspoons vanilla extract

2 cups sugar-free chocolate chips (low-carb) or Equal Exchange Organic Semi-Sweet Chocolate Chips (these chocolate chips contain sugar which is safe for Paleo but not low-carb)

1 cup chopped pecans or walnuts

PREPARATION AND INSTRUCTIONS

Preheat oven to 375° F.

Measure the almond meal, vanilla whey protein, baking soda, baking powder, and salt, and stir together. Set aside.

Using an electric mixer, beat the butter until creamy and fluffy. Add the Swerve, stevia extract, and yacon syrup, and beat until very well combined. Scrape down the sides of the bowl as needed.

Add the eggs and vanilla, and beat well.

Now add the dry ingredients, in three additions, beating each addition until well incorporated before adding the next.

Beat in the chocolate chips and pecans, and mix just until well-distributed.

Turn off mixer, and scrape the dough off the beaters back into the bowl.

Scoop dough by rounded tablespoonful onto cookie sheets you've sprayed with non-stick cooking spray, or covered with pan liners or baking parchment.

Bake cookies for 10-12 minutes. Cool on wire racks.

NUTRITIONAL INFO

I got 44 cookies, each with: 122 Calories; 10g Fat (69.0% calories from fat); 5g Protein; 4g Carbohydrate; 3g Dietary Fiber; 1g Usable Carb.

NOTES

At this writing, my beloved Nevada Manna sugar-free chocolate chips are unavailable, though I'm hoping they make a comeback. In the meanwhile, Hershey's is now making sugar-free semi-sweet chips (carbsmart.com/go/gfsf-048.php); I buy mine three bags at a time through Amazon.com (carbsmart.com/go/gfsf-048.php). Friends are starting to talk about Lily's Sugar-Free Dark Chocolate Premium Baking Chips (carbsmart.com/go/gfsf-047.php) You can also chop up sugar-free dark chocolate bars in your food processor; I did it for years and it works well. Just break them up into your processor and pulse until the bits are the right size.

If you don't want to use the yacon syrup–it's pricey, no question–you can use 1 tablespoon dark molasses, instead. It raises the carb count all the way to 5 grams per cookie, with 3 grams of fiber, for a Usable Carb count of 2 grams.

Caitlin's Paleo Chocolate Chip Cookies

by Caitlin Weeks

Low-Carb, Gluten-Free, Paleo, Vegetarian, Dairy-Free, Contains Nuts

Cooking with coconut flour is a real challenge and I made these cookies 5 times before I got them right! Almond flour is much more forgiving for gluten-free baking but I wanted a mixture that would create the right texture. I had many happy taste testers with this recipe so I hope you enjoy it!

Prep time: 10 minutes

Cooking time: 12-15 minutes

Serves: 18 cookies

INGREDIENTS

3 eggs

½ cup palm shortening (carbsmart.com/go/gfsf-073.php) or softened butter

1 teaspoon vanilla extract

½ teaspoon cinnamon

½ teaspoon nutmeg

¾ cup birch xylitol or 1 teaspoon stevia powder extract

⅓ cup coconut flour (carbsmart.com/go/gfsf-032.php)

½ teaspoon baking soda

½ teaspoon sea salt

1 cup almond meal

4 ounces unsweetened dark chocolate (carbsmart.com/go/gfsf-049.php) chopped

PREPARATION AND INSTRUCTIONS

Preheat the oven to 350° F.

Mix the eggs, palm shortening or butter, vanilla, cinnamon, nutmeg, and sweetener in a large bowl.

Sift the coconut flour into a small bowl then add the baking soda, salt, and almond flour.

Combine the two mixtures and add the chocolate chunks.

Place parchment paper on cookie sheets.

Spoon the dough on the cookie sheet in 1-inch mounds.

Bake for 15-17 minutes until browned.

NUTRITIONAL INFO

Serves 18; Per Serving: 148 Calories; 11.8g Fat (106 calories from fat); 41mg Cholesterol; 100mg Sodium; 2.7g Protein; 7.5g Carbohydrate; 1.9g Dietary Fiber; 5.6g Usable Carbs.

Dana's Peanut Butter Cookies

by Dana Carpender

Low-Carb, Gluten-Free, Vegetarian, Contains Nuts

Prep time: 10 minutes

Cooking time: 10-12 minutes

Serves: 50 cookies

INGREDIENTS

½ cup butter, softened

½ cup granular Swerve

½ teaspoon English toffee flavor liquid stevia extract

1 tablespoon yacon syrup

1 egg

1 cup natural peanut butter

½ teaspoon salt

½ teaspoon baking soda

½ teaspoon vanilla extract

¾ cup almond meal

½ cup vanilla whey protein powder

PREPARATION AND INSTRUCTIONS

Preheat oven to 375° F. Grease cookie sheets, or spray with non-stick cooking spray, or line with baking parchment.

Using an electric mixer, beat the butter until fluffy. Beat in the Swerve, stevia extract, and yacon syrup, scraping down the sides of the bowl now and then, until it's well-blended.

Now beat in the egg, peanut butter, salt, baking soda, and vanilla extract.

Add the almond meal and vanilla whey gradually, alternating additions (add about ⅓ of the almond meal, then about ⅓ of the vanilla whey, etc.), until it's all blended in.

Using clean hands, make small balls of the dough and place on prepared cookie sheets. Press flat with a fork, making crisscross marks.

Bake for 10-12 minutes.

NUTRITIONAL INFO

About 50 cookies, each with: 65 Calories; 5g Fat (66.0% calories from fat); 4g Protein; 2g Carbohydrate; trace Dietary Fiber; 2g Usable Carbs.

Paleo "Peanut Butter" Cookie

by Caitlin Weeks

Low-Carb, Gluten-Free, Paleo, Vegetarian, Dairy-Free, Contains Nuts

Peanuts have a mold called aflatoxin that has been studied as a carcinogen. Peanuts are technically a legume that contain lectins and phytates and cause digestive irritation. Traditionally, people soaked and sprouted beans, nuts, and seeds to reduce hard to digest properties but that has fallen out of fashion in our fast-paced culture. You can easily soak your almonds overnight then grind them to reduce anti-nutrients.

Prep time: 10 minutes

Cooking time: 15 minutes

Serves: 6 (12-15 cookies)

INGREDIENTS

1 cup almond butter, smooth or chunky

2 eggs

¼ cup coconut flour

½ teaspoon baking soda

½ cup birch xylitol or 2 teaspoon stevia powder extract

½ teaspoon vanilla extract

½ teaspoon sea salt

PREPARATION AND INSTRUCTIONS

Preheat the oven to 350° F.

Mix the almond butter and eggs, then sift in the coconut flour and baking soda.

Mix in the xylitol, vanilla, and salt.

When the mixture is well combined, spoon 1-inch mounds onto a parchment paper covering a cookie sheet.

Take a fork and press the down on the top of the dough to make an indentation.

Bake for 15 minutes.

NUTRITIONAL INFO

Serves 6; Per Serving (about 2 cookies): 327 Calories; 25.7g Fat (231 calories from fat); 11.7g Protein; 55mg Cholesterol; 320mg Sodium; 13.5g Carbohydrate; 3.2g Dietary Fiber; 10.3g Usable Carbs.

Almond Shortbread Cookies

by Dana Carpender

Low-Carb, Gluten-Free, Paleo (optional), Vegetarian, Contains Nuts

These buttery, easy to make Almond Shortbread Cookies are wonderful with a cup of tea!

Prep time: 15 minutes

Cooking time: 30 minutes

Yield: 48 cookies

INGREDIENTS

2 cups almond meal

½ teaspoon salt

¼ teaspoon baking powder

1 cup vanilla whey protein powder

1 cup butter, softened or extra virgin coconut oil

⅓ cup powdered Swerve

¼ teaspoon French Vanilla liquid stevia extract

1 egg

1 tablespoon water

PREPARATION AND INSTRUCTIONS

Preheat oven to 325° F. Line a jellyroll pan with baking parchment.

In a bowl, combine the almond meal, salt, baking powder, and vanilla whey protein. Stir together well.

In a mixing bowl, using an electric mixer, beat the butter until it's fluffy. While the mixer is running, add the Swerve a couple of tablespoons at a time, and beat it in. Now, with the mixer still running, drip in the stevia, a few drops at a time.

Keep that mixer going! Add the egg to the butter, and beat it in well. Now add the almond meal mixture in three or four additions, beating each in before adding another.

Finally, beat in the water. At this point, you should have a soft, sticky dough. Turn it out into your parchment-lined jellyroll pan.

Cover the dough with another sheet of parchment, and use your hands to press and pat the dough out to evenly cover the jellyroll pan.

Carefully peel off the top sheet of parchment, and score the dough into squares using a knife with a straight, thin blade–don't slice, just lay the edge of the blade on the dough and press down.

Bake for 30 minutes, or until golden.

Re-score the lines, again with a straight up-and-down motion, then let the shortbread cool a little before removing it from the parchment to a snap-top container.

NUTRITIONAL INFO

Per Serving (1 cookie): 77 Calories; 5g Fat (59.4% calories from fat); 6g Protein; 2g Carbohydrate; trace Dietary Fiber; 20mg Cholesterol; 65mg Sodium.

NOTES

What could be better than Almond Shortbread Cookies and a cup of tea? How about Almond Shortbread Cookies with a ketogenic Vanilla Toffee Coffee (page 43) topped with Coconut Milk Whipped Cream (page 90).

Macadamia Nut Biscotti

by Caitlin Weeks

Low-Carb, Gluten-Free, Paleo, Vegetarian, Vegan, Dairy-Free, Contains Nuts

My husband and I love macadamia nuts because they are so decadent. We usually buy them at Costco and then fight over them until they are gone. Macadamia nuts have a very healthy ratio of anti-inflammatory fats.

Prep time: 60 minutes

Cooking time: 20 minutes

Serves: 12

INGREDIENTS

2 eggs

1½ cups almond meal

½ cup coconut flour

¾ cup birch xylitol or 1 teaspoon stevia powder extract

½ teaspoon baking soda

¼ teaspoon sea salt

1 teaspoon vanilla extract

½ cup macadamia nuts (carbsmart.com/go/gfsf-057.php), roughly chopped

PREPARATION AND INSTRUCTIONS

Preheat oven to 350° F.

Put eggs, almond flour, coconut flour, xylitol, baking soda, and salt in your food processor and pulse until combined.

With the machine running, add the eggs and vanilla extract and let the mixture blend well.

You will end up with thick and pasty dough.

Scrape the dough from the food processor into a large bowl.

Work the macadamias into the dough with a spatula or using your hands.

Line a baking sheet with parchment paper and turn out the dough.

Form the dough into a rectangle shape that is no more than 1 inch tall.

Bake the dough for 15 minutes, then turn the oven off and leave them inside for 20 minutes.

Cut the biscotti into twelve 1-inch thick slices and lay them face up.

Turn the oven back on 350° F.

Put the slices back in the oven for 5 minutes to crisp, then turn the oven off again and leave them inside for 15 minutes.

Let them cool then serve with coffee or tea.

NUTRITIONAL INFO

Serves 12; Per Serving: 162 Calories; 11.6g Fat (104 calories from fat); 0mg Cholesterol; 98mg Sodium; 4.5g Protein; 9g Carbohydrate; 3.7g Dietary Fiber; 5.3g Usable Carbs.

Pecan Sandies

by Caitlin Weeks

Low-Carb, Gluten-Free, Paleo, Dairy-Free, Vegetarian, Contains Nuts

As a child, my father's favorite cookie was a Pecan Sandie, so I tried to make these to see if he could tell the difference. I was so excited to see his face when he tried my cookies. He said they were even better than he remembered.

Prep time: 10 minutes

Cooking time: 15 minutes

Serves: 6 (makes 15-18 cookies)

INGREDIENTS

1 cup softened coconut oil

2 eggs

¾ teaspoon stevia powder extract
or ¼ cup birch xylitol

1 teaspoon vanilla extract

¾ cup coconut flour

¼ cup almond flour

½ teaspoon baking soda

¾ cup pecans, chopped

PREPARATION AND INSTRUCTIONS

Heat oven to 350° F.

Mix coconut oil, eggs, and vanilla extract in a bowl.

Sift the coconut flour and mix the other dry ingredients except pecans in another bowl.

Combine the two mixtures thoroughly.

Mix in the pecans at the end with your hands.

Scoop the dough into 1-inch balls and place on a cookie sheet covered with parchment paper.

Cook for 12-15 minutes until cooked through.

NUTRITIONAL INFO

Serves 6; Per Serving (about 2 cookies): 551 Calories; 52.7g Fat (475 calories from fat); 55mg Cholesterol; 131mg Sodium; 7.1g Protein; 12.7g Carbohydrate; 6.8g Dietary Fiber; 5.9g Usable Carbs.

Coconut and Cinnamon Keto Fat Bombs

By Caitlin Weeks

Low-Carb, Gluten-Free, Paleo, Ketogenic, Dairy-Free, Vegetarian

I made these coconut ketosis low-carb fat bombs over the holidays for family. They are decadent bon bons that are great for taking to a party or as a late night snack. Coconut is easy to digest and preferentially burned as energy not stored as fat. This recipe is perfect for a ketogenic and low-carb plan. People who are more Paleo inclined may want to add honey instead of stevia if carbs are not a concern. You can whip up this easy recipe and have everyone ooohing and aahhing in no time.

Prep time: 10 minutes

Cook time: 5 minutes

Serves 10-12 balls

INGREDIENTS

1 cup coconut butter (carbsmart.com/go/gfsf-063.php)–almond butter may also work, coconut oil will not work

1 cup full fat coconut milk (Do not use low-fat version from a box!!!)

1 teaspoon gluten-free vanilla extract

½ teaspoon nutmeg

½ teaspoon cinnamon

1 teaspoon stevia powder extract

1 cup coconut shreds

PREPARATION AND INSTRUCTIONS

Place a glass bowl over a saucepan with a few inches of water in it to create a double boiler.

Place all the ingredients except shredded coconut in the glass bowl over medium heat.

Mix the ingredients while waiting for them to melt.

When all the ingredients are combined remove the bowl from the heat.

Place the bowl in the fridge until it is hard enough to roll into balls, about 30 minutes.

Roll the contents into 1-inch balls and roll them through the coconut shreds.

Place the balls on a plate and refrigerate for one hour.

Serve and enjoy. Keep refrigerated when not serving.

NUTRITIONAL INFO

Serving Size 1 ball; Per Serving: 238 Calories; 25g Fat (91.9% calories from fat); 1g Protein; 0mg Cholesterol; 19mg Sodium; 4g Carbohydrate; 1g Dietary Fiber; 3g Usable Carbs.

Cakes and Pies

Coconut pie, peach cobbler, vanilla muffins, and moist brownies are just a few of the things you might find in the bakery of your dreams. All this and more made even better because every one of these scrumptious cakes and pies you find in this section are free of sugars and grains. Good for the body and great for the soul!

Crustless Coconut Pie

by Dana Carpender

Low-Carb, Gluten-Free, Paleo (optional), Ketogenic, Vegetarian, Nut-Free

This pie is great the way it is–and fits Fat Fast parameters, if you're Fat Fasting. (See Fat Fast Cookbook (carbsmart.com/go/gfsf-051.php)–for more on Fat Fasting.) But it also makes a great base for all kinds of toppings. We first tried it with CarbSmart Vanilla Ice Cream (available in your grocer's freezer) and sugar-free chocolate sauce; it was amazing. We've spread it with a little Polaner low-sugar, high fiber preserves (carbsmart.com/go/gfsf-052.php) for breakfast. How about sliced strawberries and whipped cream, for a great low-carb version of strawberry shortcake? The possibilities are endless.

Prep time: 10 minutes

Cooking time: 50-60 minutes

Serves: 12

INGREDIENTS

4 eggs

1 pint heavy cream or 16 ounces full fat coconut milk

½ cup granular Swerve

¼ teaspoon French vanilla liquid stevia extract

1 teaspoon vanilla extract

¼ teaspoon salt

2 tablespoons butter or extra-virgin coconut oil, melted

¼ teaspoon baking powder

1 cup shredded coconut meat (carbsmart.com/go/gfsf-036.php)

PREPARATION AND INSTRUCTIONS

Preheat oven to 350° F.

Grease a 10" pie plate, or coat with non-stick cooking spray.

Put everything but the coconut in your blender, and run until it's all well-blended.

Put the coconut in your pie plate, and pour the custard mixture over it.

Stir carefully to mix the coconut into the custard. (Why not just put the coconut in the blender? I tried it; the mixture was too thick, and the coconut didn't blend in.)

Bake for 50-60 minutes, until browned and set. Cool, then chill.

NUTRITIONAL INFO

12 servings, each with: 200 Calories; 20g Fat (89.6% calories from fat); 122mg Cholesterol; 109mg Sodium; 3g Protein; 2g Carbohydrate; 1g Dietary Fiber; 1g Usable Carb.

NOTES

Try drizzling some of Caitlin's Chocolate Syrup (page 96) on top for an extra tasty treat!

Easy Dairy-Free Coconut Custard Pie

by Caitlin Weeks

Low-Carb, Gluten-Free, Paleo, Vegetarian, Dairy-Free, Contains Nuts

My Grandma makes a coconut pie in her blender with regular flour and it was always my favorite. I recreated her recipe using gluten-free and Paleo ingredients. I am crazy about coconut and I hope you like it too!

Prep time: 5 minutes

Cooking time: 60 minutes

Serves: 8

INGREDIENTS

2 cups full fat coconut milk, canned

¾ cup birch xylitol or 3 teaspoons stevia powder extract

3 eggs

1 dash salt

1 teaspoons vanilla

½ cup almond meal

1 cup shredded coconut

PREPARATION AND INSTRUCTIONS

Preheat oven to 350° F.

Mix all the ingredients except shredded coconut in the blender.

Add the coconut shreds and pulse a few more times.

Pour into a pie plate and bake for 50-60 minutes.

NUTRITIONAL INFO

Serves 8; Per Serving Size 92.3g; 291 Calories; 21g Fat (115 calories from fat); 80mg Cholesterol; 60mg Sodium 7g Protein; 29g Carbohydrate; 20g Dietary Fiber; 9g Usable Carbs.

Peach Cobbler

by Dana Carpender

Low-Carb, Gluten-Free, Paleo (optional), Vegetarian, Contains Nuts

Feel free to make this with blueberries or blackberries, instead. Try serving this warm with a scoop of CarbSmart vanilla ice cream (available in your grocer's freezer) on top!

Prep time: 15 minutes

Cooking time: 30 minutes

Serves: 9

INGREDIENTS

4 cups sliced peaches

¼ cup plus 1 tablespoon powdered Swerve

½ teaspoon plus ¼ teaspoon liquid stevia extract–plain is good, but lemon would be good, too.

1½ tablespoons lemon juice

8 tablespoons butter, divided

½ cup almond meal

½ cup vanilla whey protein powder

2½ teaspoons corn-free baking powder

1 teaspoon salt

½ cup heavy cream or full fat coconut milk

PREPARATION AND INSTRUCTIONS

Preheat oven to 375° F. Spray an 8" x 8" baking pan with non-stick cooking spray, or grease with coconut oil.

In a mixing bowl, combine the sliced peaches (I use unsweetened, frozen peach slices–saves lots of time and trouble, and since they're going to be cooked, it makes no difference in the final texture), with ¼ cup Swerve. Stir the liquid stevia extract into the lemon juice, then sprinkle it over the peaches. Toss everything together, and spread evenly in the pan. Dot with 2 tablespoons of the butter.

In another mixing bowl (or heck, go ahead and use the same one if you like) combine the almond meal, vanilla whey, baking powder, the one tablespoon of Swerve, and the salt. Stir together to evenly distribute ingredients.

Melt the remaining 6 tablespoons of butter. Measure the cream, and stir the butter into it, along with the second stevia extract. Pour into the dry ingredients, and mix with a few swift strokes of your whisk or a spoon–you just want to stir enough to insure that there are no pockets of dry ingredients lurking.

Spread the batter evenly over the peaches, and bake for 30 minutes, or until the crust is crisp and evenly golden brown. Serve warm.

NUTRITIONAL INFO

9 servings, each with: 250 Calories; 17g Fat (60.0% calories from fat); 14g Protein; 13g Carbohydrate; 2g Dietary Fiber; 11g Usable Carbs.

Strawberry Cheesecake Bars

by Dana Carpender

Low-Carb, Gluten-Free, Contains Nuts

A friend posted a recipe for a dessert with a strawberry-gelatin-and-cream cheese topping on a pretzel crust. Never one to let such a challenge go by, I promptly decarbed it. Fabulous!

Prep time: 25 minutes

Cooking time: 30 minutes

Serves: 12

INGREDIENTS

2 cups almond meal

¼ cup vanilla whey protein powder

½ cup powdered Swerve

1 tablespoon coarse salt

½ cup butter, melted

½ cup heavy cream

12 ounces cream cheese, room temperature

3 tablespoons half and half

½ teaspoon French Vanilla liquid stevia extract

1½ pounds strawberries, hulled

1½ cups water

2 tablespoons lemon juice

1½ tablespoons plain gelatin powder (carbsmart.com/go/gfsf-054.php)

½ teaspoon liquid stevia extract, or as needed. I used plain, but lemon would be good, too.

PREPARATION AND INSTRUCTIONS

Preheat oven to 350° F. Grease or spray a 9" x 13" pan, or line it with non-stick aluminum foil–this looks really pretty in a Pyrex baking dish.

In your food processor, combine the almond meal, vanilla whey protein powder, and Swerve. Pulse to combine. Add the salt and the butter, and pulse just until the butter is evenly worked in–you don't want to break down the salt crystals too much.

Turn this mixture into your prepared pan and press it out into an even layer. Bake for 15 minutes, or until evenly golden. Cool.

When your crust has cooled, you are ready to continue. In a deep bowl, with an electric mixer, whip the heavy cream until stiff. Don't overbeat, or you'll get butter!

In another bowl, using the same mixer–no need to wash it first–beat together the cream cheese, half and half, and French Vanilla liquid stevia extract. Scrape down the sides of the bowl often, and beat until everything's well-combined and fluffy.

Using a rubber scraper, fold the whipped cream into the cream cheese mixture. When the whipped cream is well-incorporated, spread the cheese mixture evenly over the crust.

Put your strawberries, water, and lemon juice in a non-reactive saucepan, and sprinkle the gelatin powder evenly over the top.

Over medium heat, bring to a low simmer. Cook for about 15 minutes, or until the berries are soft. Mash them up a bit with a fork or whisk, but don't completely puree them.

Stir in the liquid stevia extract, and taste–whether you need more will depend on how sweet your berries are naturally, and how sweet you like stuff.

Spread the sweetened strawberry mixture evenly over the cream cheese layer. Cover the whole thing with foil–not touching the strawberries–and chill for at least several hours, and overnight is better.

Cut in squares to serve.

NUTRITIONAL INFO

12 servings, each with: 338 Calories; 26g Fat (67.5% calories from fat); 16g Protein; 12g Carbohydrate; 1g Dietary Fiber; 11g Usable Carbs.

NOTES

Feel free to make this with raspberries instead–if you can afford that many raspberries!

Choco-Peanut Flourless Cakes

by Dana Carpender

Low-Carb, Gluten-Free, Paleo (optional), Vegetarian, Contains Nuts

These Choco-Peanut Flourless Cakes are decadent!! Rich and creamy, they will satisfy even the most discerning chocoholic.

Prep time: 15 minutes

Cooking time: 35 minutes

Serves: 8

INGREDIENTS

6 tablespoons butter or <u>extra virgin coconut oil</u>

1 cup (6 ounces) <u>sugar-free chocolate chips</u> (low-carb) or <u>Equal Exchange Organic Semi-Sweet Chocolate Chips</u> (these chocolate chips contain sugar which is safe for Paleo but not low-carb)

⅓ cup natural peanut butter or almond butter

6 eggs, separated

1 pinch cream of tartar

⅔ cup <u>powdered Swerve</u>

PREPARATION AND INSTRUCTIONS

Preheat oven to 325° F. Grease or spray 8 big custard cups or 6-7 ounce ramekins. Place them all in a shallow pan for ease of handling.

Melt the butter, chocolate, and peanut butter together–I put mine in a glass bowl and nuke 'em for a minute, stir, and give 'em another 30 seconds. When it's all melted, whisk it together well.

Let that cool a minute or two while you separate your eggs. Be aware that even the tiniest speck of yolk will keep your whites from whipping, so do yourself a favor and separate each white into a custard cup before transferring it to a larger, deep bowl for whipping. If you get a little yolk in one, save it for scrambling later, and wash and dry your custard cup before continuing with your separating.

Once your eggs are separated, whisk the yolks into the chocolate mixture one at a time.

Now to whip your whites. You can use a whisk if you like, but I find an electric mixer easier. Add the cream of tartar, and using the high speed of the beater, start whipping your whites. When they're getting stiff, add the Swerve and beat until glossy.

Add about ⅓ of the beaten white to the chocolate mixture and stir it in. Now add the chocolate mixture to the rest of the beaten whites, and fold in gently, using a rubber scraper.

Divide the batter between your prepared custard cups or ramekins–I used my cookie scoop so I could divide the mixture evenly, but that's hardly essential. Just divide the batter as evenly as you can.

Bake for 35 minutes.

Serve warm with CarbSmart vanilla ice cream (available in your grocer's freezer).

NUTRITIONAL INFO

8 servings, each with: 345 Calories; 27g Fat (69.3% calories from fat); 8g Protein; 18g Carbohydrate; 14g Dietary Fiber; 4g Usable Carbs.

Easy Vanilla Muffin

by Caitlin Weeks

Low-Carb, Gluten-Free, Paleo, Vegetarian, Dairy-Free, Nut-Free

This one is great muffin because it can be breakfast or a snack. It is perfectly portable to take to work or eat on the go. Unlike most muffins it is full of protein and healthy fats that will satisfy.

Prep time: 5 minutes

Cooking time: 15 minutes

Serves: 4 (Makes 4 muffins)

INGREDIENTS

¼ cup full fat coconut milk, canned

4 eggs

1 teaspoon gluten free vanilla extract

2 tablespoons coconut flour

1 teaspoon cinnamon

½ teaspoon nutmeg

¼ teaspoon salt

¼ teaspoon baking soda

1 teaspoon stevia powder extract

PREPARATION AND INSTRUCTIONS

Preheat the oven to 350° F.

Mix the wet ingredient in one bowl.

Sift the coconut flour and then mix the dry ingredients.

Combine the two mixtures until smooth.

Pour into lined muffin cups.

Bake for 15 minutes.

NUTRITIONAL INFO

Serves 4; Per Serving: 120 Calories; 8.6g Fat (77 calories from fat); 164mg Cholesterol; 292mg Sodium; 6.7g Protein; 4.3g Carbohydrate; 1.9g Dietary Fiber; 2.4g Usable Carbs.

Cinnamon "Apple" Crisp

by Caitlin Weeks

Low-Carb, Gluten-Free, Paleo. Vegetarian, Vegan (if coconut oil is used), Contains Nuts

I first made this with my sister when we were visiting my Grandpa. He did not even know that he was eating something healthy and low-carb. He even asked for seconds. This can be made with apples if someone is not so concerned with watching carbs.

Prep time: 10 minutes

Cooking time: 50 minutes

Serves: 12

INGREDIENTS

6 chayote squash

5 tablespoons birch xylitol divided

3 teaspoons cinnamon

4 tablespoons butter or coconut oil, plus 1 tablespoon for greasing the pan

½ cup chopped pistachio

1 cup sliced almonds

½ cup shredded coconut, unsweetened

PREPARATION AND INSTRUCTIONS

Preheat the oven to 350° F.

Grease a medium sized baking dish with 1 tablespoon butter or coconut oil.

Peel and cut the chayote squash into bite-sized chunks.

Mix 1 tablespoon of xylitol and 1 teaspoon of cinnamon with the squash and place into a greased baking dish.

Melt the butter or coconut oil in a saucepan and stir in the remaining xylitol and cinnamon, pistachios, almonds and coconut shreds.

Once the mixture is well combined pour over the squash, making sure it is distributed evenly.

Bake for 30 minutes covered with foil, then uncover and cook for 15-20 more minutes to crisp the top.

NUTRITIONAL INFO

Serves 12; ½ cup Per Serving: 157 Calories; 13.3g Fat (118 calories from fat); 3.4g Protein; 0mg Cholesterol; 10mg Sodium; 8.8g Carbohydrate; 2.7g Dietary Fiber; 6.1g Usable Carbs.

Red Velvet Cupcakes

by Caitlin Weeks

Low-Carb, Gluten-Free, Paleo, Vegetarian, Dairy-Free Option

In my mind, Red Velvet Cake is something from a cheap supermarket bakery, so I wanted to take it up a notch with this healthier version. I added many nutrient-dense ingredients to class up this cake. The beets will turn it red but if you want it to be really crimson try the natural food coloring suggestion.

Prep time: 10 minutes

Cooking time: 20 minutes

Serves: 6

INGREDIENTS

4 eggs

⅓ cup beets, finely grated

⅓ cup palm shortening or softened butter

½ cup birch xylitol or
2 teaspoons stevia powder extract

¼ cup coconut flour

¼ cup cocoa powder

½ teaspoon baking soda

¼ teaspoon sea salt

1 teaspoon natural
India Tree red food coloring
(carbsmart.com/go/gfsf-056.php)

PREPARATION AND INSTRUCTIONS

Preheat the oven to 350° F.

Mix the wet ingredients.

Sift the coconut flour and cocoa powder then mix in the rest of the dry ingredients.

Combine the two mixtures and stir well.

Pour into lined muffin tins and bake for 17-20 minutes.

Let them cool off then ice with **White Icing Recipe (page 73).**

NUTRITIONAL INFO

Serves 6; Per Serving: 462 Calories; 47.3g Fat (426 calories from fat); 0mg Cholesterol; 204mg Sodium; 1.6g Protein; 11.1g Carbohydrate; 3g Dietary Fiber; 8.1g Usable Carbs.

White Icing Recipe

by Caitlin Weeks

Low-Carb, Gluten-Free, Paleo (optional), Vegetarian, Dairy-Free, Vegan, Nut-free

Nothing tops off the perfect cupcake like a sinfully delicious icing! This one is not only scrumptious but quilt free. Enjoy on my red velvet cupcakes or your favorite cake.

Prep time: 5 minutes

Cooking time: NA

Serves: 6

INGREDIENTS

1 cup palm shortening or softened butter

1 teaspoons stevia powder extract or ¼ cup birch xylitol

½ teaspoon vanilla extract

PREPARATION AND INSTRUCTIONS

Mix all the ingredients with a hand mixer for 2-3 minutes until fluffy.

Wait until the cupcakes are cool then ice generously.

NUTRITIONAL INFO

Serves 6; Per Serving: 69 Calories; 6g Fat (43 calories from fat); 0mg Cholesterol; 0mg Sodium; 0g Protein; 8g Carbohydrate; 8g Dietary Fiber; 0g Usable Carbs.

Strawberry Shortcake

by Caitlin Weeks

Low-Carb, Gluten-Free, Paleo, Vegetarian, Dairy-Free, Contains Nuts

My parents used to make strawberry shortcake in the summer time and top with Cool Whip. I would sneak off and eat the whole tub when no one was watching. I am so glad I now know that heavy whipping cream is so much healthier than cool whip. For optimal long-term health, artificial and man-made ingredients should be avoided.

Prep time: 5 minutes

Cooking time: N/A

Serves: 6

INGREDIENTS

1 teaspoon rose water (carbsmart.com/go/gfsf-077.php) or ½ teaspoon grated lemon zest

1 teaspoon vanilla extract

6 eggs

½ cup melted coconut oil

¼ cup coconut flour

¼ cup almond flour

½ teaspoon sea salt

½ teaspoon baking soda

½ cup birch xylitol or 2 teaspoons stevia powder extract

3 cups sliced strawberries

PREPARATION AND INSTRUCTIONS

Preheat the oven to 350° F.

Mix the rose water, vanilla, eggs, and coconut oil.

Sift in the coconut flour, and then mix in the almond flour, salt, baking soda, and sweetener.

Line muffin cup with liners; fill them with batter about ⅔ full.

Bake for 35 minutes then cool on a rack until room temperature.

Slice them open and top with sliced strawberries.

Add whipping cream or Coconut Milk Whipped Cream (page 90) as desired (not in nutrition info).

NUTRITIONAL INFO

Serves 6; Per Serving: 314 Calories; 25.4g Fat (229 calories from fat); 8g Protein; 164mg Cholesterol; 325mg Sodium; 12.8g Carbohydrate; 3.1g Dietary Fiber; 9.7g Usable Carbs.

Macadamia Nut Pie Crust

by Caitlin Weeks

Low-Carb, Gluten-Free, Paleo, Vegetarian, Dairy-Free, Contains Nuts

The first time I made this crust, I used almonds. It seemed rather dull so I wanted to make it more exciting. What could be more interesting and rich than a low-carb crust made with macadamia nuts? If you're strapped for cash, almonds can be substituted.

Prep time: 10 minutes

Cooking time: 20 minutes

Serves: 6

INGREDIENTS

¾ cups macadamia nuts

1 cup almond flour

1 egg

½ teaspoon salt

½ teaspoon stevia powder extract

PREPARATION AND INSTRUCTIONS

Preheat the oven to 350° F.

Pulse the macadamia nuts in a food processor until fine.

Transfer the macadamia nuts into a mixing bowl and add in the almond flour, egg, salt, and stevia, then mix with your hands.

Transfer the dough into a pie plate and press along the sides until the pie plate is covered evenly.

Bake for 8-10 minutes.

Let the crust cool before adding any filling.

NUTRITIONAL INFO

Serves 6; Per Serving: 251 Calories; 23.4g Fat (211 calories from fat); 2.2g Protein; 27mg Cholesterol; 205mg Sodium; 5.7g Carbohydrate; 3.4g Dietary Fiber; 2.3g Usable Carbs.

Key Lime Pie

by Caitlin Weeks

Low-Carb, Gluten-Free, Paleo, Vegetarian, Crust Contains Nuts

My dad's favorite pie is Key Lime Pie but I had never made it in my life until recently. I made this one with him in mind. I live 3,000 miles away from my dad but my husband gave this Key Lime Pie his stamp of approval. Hope you feel like you are on a vacation while eating this refreshing treat.

Prep time: 10 minutes

Cooking time: 20 minutes

Serves: 6

INGREDIENTS

6 eggs

2 cups full fat <u>coconut milk</u>, canned

½ cup lime juice

Zest of 3 medium limes

½ teaspoon <u>stevia powder extract</u>

¼ cup <u>birch xylitol</u>

1 tablespoon arrowroot flour

1 <u>Macadamia Nut Pie Crust (page 75)</u>

PREPARATION AND INSTRUCTIONS

Whisk all the ingredients in a glass mixing bowl except the arrowroot flour.

Heat up a few inches of water in a saucepan over medium heat.

Put the glass bowl over the saucepan making sure the water does not touch the bottom of the bowl.

Keep mixing until the mixture starts to thicken–about 10 minutes.

When the mixture starts to thicken, sift in the arrowroot flour and stir until mixed.

Pour the pie filling into the cooled pie crust and refrigerate for two hours.

Slice and top with <u>Coconut Milk Whipped Cream (page 90)</u>.

NUTRITIONAL INFO

Serves 6; Per Serving: 176 Calories; 16.9g Fat (152 calories from fat); 0mg Cholesterol; 11mg Sodium; 1.8g Protein; 7.7g Carbohydrate; 1.7g Dietary Fiber; 6g Usable Carbs.

Blueberry Almond Coffee Cake

by Caitlin Weeks

Low-Carb, Gluten-Free, Paleo, Vegetarian, Dairy-Free, Contains Nuts

I made this coffee cake for a friend who was traveling. She said it made her day to have a homemade coffee cake in her carry on bag. She was not even hungry for the junky food at the airport. Now, she requests it every time she comes back to visit.

Prep time: 10 minutes

Cooking time: 40 minutes

Serves: 9

INGREDIENTS

½ cup coconut flour

½ teaspoon baking soda

6 eggs

½ teaspoon vanilla extract

½ cup coconut oil, melted

⅓ cup birch xylitol
or 1 teaspoon powdered stevia extract

1 pint blueberries

¼ cup sliced almonds

PREPARATION AND INSTRUCTIONS

Preheat the oven to 350° F.

Sift the coconut flour and baking soda into a bowl.

Mix the eggs, vanilla, coconut oil, and sweetener in another bowl.

Add the two bowls together and mix well.

Fold in the blueberries and almonds carefully.

Fill a greased 8" x 8" cake pan with the batter.

Bake for 30-40 minutes until a knife inserted in the middle comes out clean.

NUTRITIONAL INFO

Serves 9; Per Serving: 239 Calories; 18.3g Fat (165 calories from fat); 6.3g Protein; 114mg Cholesterol; 119mg Sodium; 12.5g Carbohydrate; 3.5g Dietary Fiber; 9g Usable Carbs.

Moist Brownies

by Caitlin Weeks

Low-Carb, Gluten-Free, Paleo, Vegetarian, Dairy-Free, Nut-Free

These brownies have a secret ingredient that keeps them light and airy. When was the last time you tasted brownies with two servings of vegetables without even knowing it? These brownies have the benefit of filling you up without filling you out.

Prep time: 10 minutes

Cooking time: 35 minutes

Serves: 9 brownies

INGREDIENTS

1 cup canned pumpkin (carbsmart.com/go/gfsf-058.php)

½ cup plus 2 tablespoons cocoa powder

½ cup coconut oil

¼ cup birch xylitol

½ teaspoon stevia powder extract

3 eggs

1 teaspoon cinnamon

3 tablespoons coconut flour

½ teaspoon baking soda

PREPARATION AND INSTRUCTIONS

Preheat the oven to 350° F.

In a saucepan over medium heat mix the pumpkin, cocoa, coconut oil and sweeteners until well mixed.

Pour the mixture into a large bowl and add in eggs and cinnamon.

Sift in the coconut flour and baking soda and mix well.

Transfer the mixture into an 8" x 8" baking dish and bake for 30-35 minutes until a knife comes out clean.

Serve warm or cold.

NUTRITIONAL INFO

Serves 9; Per Serving: 166 Calories; 14.8g Fat (133 calories from fat); 55mg Cholesterol; 24mg Sodium; 3.8g Protein; 8.2g Carbohydrate; 3.6g Dietary Fiber; 4.6g Usable Carbs.

Cheesy Cocktail Crust

by Dana Carpender

Low-Carb, Gluten-Free, Nut-free, Vegetarian

I invented this for the Hot Ham Cocktail Pie (page 80), but it would be good for any hot appetizer pie recipe. It would also make a yummy quiche.

Prep time: 10 minutes

Cooking time: 15 minutes

Serves: 12

INGREDIENTS

4 ounces cheddar cheese

1 cup sunflower seeds
(carbsmart.com/go/gfsf-038.php)

¼ teaspoon salt

¼ teaspoon baking powder

¼ teaspoon paprika–I used smoked paprika, but use what you have on hand

2 tablespoons water

PREPARATION AND INSTRUCTIONS

Preheat oven to 350° F. Grease a 9" pie plate, or coat with non-stick cooking spray.

Run your cheddar through the shredding blade of your food processor. Remove it to a small bowl, and swap out the shredding disc for the S-blade.

Put the sunflower seeds, salt, baking powder, and paprika in the processor, and run until you have a fine meal. Scrape down the sides once or twice during this process, to make sure everything is well-blended.

Add the cheese back to the food processor and blend well with the sunflower mixture.

With the processor running, add the water a tablespoon at a time. Very quickly you'll have a mass of soft, sticky dough. Turn off the processor.

Turn the dough out into the prepared pie plate, and press it out evenly over the bottom and up the sides of the pie plate. Don't bring it up over the rim, just leave it level with the edge.

Bake for 15-17 minutes, until lightly golden. Cool before filling.

NUTRITIONAL INFO

12 servings, each with: 107 Calories; 9g Fat (73.1% calories from fat); 5g Protein; 2g Carbohydrate; 1g Dietary Fiber; 1g Usable Carb.

Hot Ham Cocktail Pie

by Dana Carpender

Low-Carb, Gluten-Free

This is a riff on a recipe my Mom used to make for cocktail parties. (Actually, she would have me make it. I was official Kitchen Help for parties.) The original recipe used packaged pie crust mix, deviled ham, and pickle relish; as you can see, I've cleaned it up quite a lot. I guess the ham has a little sugar, but if you read the labels and are choosy, it won't be much.

Prep time: 5 minutes

Cooking time: 15 minutes

Serves: 12

INGREDIENTS

1 Cheesy Cocktail Crust (page 79)

4 ounces ham

2 ounces Stevia Bread and Butter Pickles (page 39)

2 tablespoons mayonnaise

1 tablespoon bacon grease

1 tablespoon brown mustard

1 teaspoon prepared horseradish

PREPARATION AND INSTRUCTIONS

Have your crust made and pre-baked. Crank the oven up to 450° F. While that's heating...

Put everything in the food processor, and run until the ham and pickles are finely chopped, and the other ingredients are evenly blended in.

Spread this mixture evenly over the bottom of the crust. Cover the edges of the crust with strips of foil–this will keep them from burning while you bake the pie.

Bake for 15 minutes.
Serve hot, in small wedges.

NUTRITIONAL INFO

12 servings, each with: 152 Calories; 13g Fat (75.0% calories from fat); 7g Protein; 3g Carbohydrate; 1g Dietary Fiber; 2g Usable Carbs.

Sweet Treats

Satisfy any sweet tooth with delectable treats like Hibiscus Gelatin, Chocolate Mint Popsicles, "Bread" Pudding, and more! Whether you are looking for quick and easy finger foods to keep handy for the family or the perfect dessert for a dinner party, you are sure to find it here!

Hibiscus Finger Gelatin

by Dana Carpender

Low-Carb, Gluten-Free, Paleo, Dairy-Free, Nut-Free

You've had Jell-O® Jigglers or Knox Blox? Here's your alternative. Not only are they fun to eat, taste great, and give you a little nibble of something sweet, but they're full of antioxidants from the hibiscus, while cinnamon lowers blood sugar and ginger settles a queasy tummy and is traditionally used for colds. Plus they help you work more gelatin into your diet. Consider these if you're recovering from a queasy tummy!

Prep time: 10 minutes

Cooking time: 35 minutes

Yields: 117 squares

INGREDIENTS

3 cups boiling water

¾ cup dried hibiscus

2 cinnamon sticks

1 inch ginger root

liquid stevia or powdered stevia blend, to equal ⅓ cup sugar, or to taste

3 tablespoons gelatin powder, unsweetened

1 cup cold water

PREPARATION AND INSTRUCTIONS

In a pitcher or big bowl, combine the hibiscus with the cinnamon sticks and the ginger root–slice the ginger root paper thin across the grain, first. Pour the boiling water over this combination, and let it sit for 15 minutes.

Meanwhile, sprinkle the gelatin powder over 1 cup cold water. Let that sit while the hibiscus steeps. In the meanwhile, grease or spray a 9" x 13" pan.

When 15 minutes have passed, strain the hibiscus mixture, throwing the solids away. The liquid will be ruby-red, and should still be hot. First stir in the stevia, then stir in the gelatin that you've soaked in water, whisking until it's all dissolved.

Pour into the prepared pan and chill until set. When it's set, use a thin, straight bladed knife to cut in squares. If you cut 'em 1" square you'll get 117 of them, but I cut them a little bigger.

NUTRITIONAL INFO

If you make 117 squares, each will have: 2 Calories; trace Fat (5.5% calories from fat); trace Protein; trace Carbohydrate; trace Dietary Fiber.

NOTES

The recipe contains a super-sweet blend of stevia and erythritol designed to not have that bitter taste some stevia powders have, to make this recipe, and it worked extremely well. It's simply called Stevia (Reb A) and Erythritol by Natural Mate (carbsmart.com/go/gfsf-025.php) I'll be trying this sweetener in more applications.

Easy Vanilla Chia Pudding

by Caitlin Weeks

Low-Carb, Gluten-Free, Paleo, Vegetarian, Vegan, Dairy-Free, Nut-Free

This is an easy pudding that can be made in a snap when you have a sweet craving. I make it all the time when I want something sweet without a lot of hassle. If you are impatient, place the pudding in the freezer to speed up the process.

Prep time: 1 hour

Cooking time: N/A

Serves: 4

INGREDIENTS

5 tablespoons chia seeds (carbsmart.com/go/gfsf-030.php)

2 cups full fat coconut milk, canned

½ teaspoon vanilla extract

½ teaspoon stevia powder extract

PREPARATION AND INSTRUCTIONS

Grind the chia in a coffee grinder or use ground chia so you don't have to use the coffee grinder.

Stir all the ingredients together let them sit in the fridge 1 hour to chill.

CHOCOLATE VARIATION

Add 4 tablespoons of cocoa powder for a chocolate pudding (will add 4 net carbs total).

NUTRITIONAL INFO

Serves 4; ½ cup Per Serving: 312 Calories; 31.7g Fat (286 calories from fat); 0mg Cholesterol; 18mg Sodium; 4.6g Protein; 10.9g Carbohydrate; 5.8g Dietary Fiber; 5.1g Usable Carbs.

Chocolate Almond Cups

by Caitlin Weeks

Low-Carb, Gluten-Free, Paleo, Vegetarian, Vegan, Contains Nuts

I grew up eating way too many chocolate peanut butter cups from the grocery store. The conventional kind are full of processed and genetically modified ingredients. I wanted to see if I could make them at home with natural ingredients without compromising on taste. I think this recipe is even better than the original because I used almond butter and they are guilt-free.

Prep time: 60 minutes

Cooking time: N/A

Serves: 10 (Makes approximately10 cups)

INGREDIENTS

5 ounces <u>unsweetened dark chocolate</u>

½ cup full fat <u>coconut milk</u>, canned

1 teaspoon <u>stevia powder extract</u> or ¼ cup <u>birch xylitol</u>

½ teaspoon gluten-free vanilla extract

¼ cup almond butter, chilled

PREPARATION AND INSTRUCTIONS

Melt the chocolate over a double boiler then add the coconut milk, stevia or xylitol, and vanilla.

Mix until blended then put half of the chocolate into lined mini muffin cups.

Chill the chocolate for 15 minutes.

Use a small spoon to place the chilled almond butter in the middle of the chocolate.

Leave a little space around the almond butter so that the bottom chocolate is exposed.

Add another spoonful of the chocolate on top to cover the almond butter, making sure the top chocolate meets the bottom chocolate to seal in the almond butter.

Chill for 45 minutes in the refrigerator then enjoy.

NUTRITIONAL INFO

Serves 10; 1 cup Per Serving: 135 Calories; 11g Fat (99 calories from fat); 2g Protein; 0mg Cholesterol; 4mg Sodium; 11g Carbohydrate; 1g Dietary Fiber; 10g Usable Carbs.

Lime Gelatin Jigglers

by Caitlin Weeks

Low-Carb, Gluten-Free, Paleo, Dairy-Free, Egg-Free, Nut-Free

These tart, lime, gummy treats are fun for the young and young at heart. They will remind you of a lime aid on a hot day. Limes are full of vitamin C, which help boost the immune system. For a change of pace, try lemons in the recipe.

Prep time: 1 hour

Cooking time 5 min

Serves 2 (makes 12-15 shapes)

INGREDIENTS

2 cups water

8 tablespoons gelatin (Great Lakes, orange can, beef)

Juice from 2 medium limes

2 teaspoon lime zest

¼ cup birch xylitol or 1 teaspoon stevia powder extract

PREPARATION AND INSTRUCTIONS

Heat up the water over medium heat and stir in the gelatin until dissolved.

Remove the gelatin from heat and mix in the lime juice, zest, and sweetener.

Pour into molds or mini muffin cups.

Refrigerate for one hour until chilled and enjoy.

NUTRITIONAL INFO

Serves 2; Per Serving (about 6 jigglers): 122 Calories; 0.1g Fat (1 calories from fat); 164mg Cholesterol; 63mg Sodium; 24.1g Protein; 7.9g Carbohydrate; 0g Dietary Fiber; 7.9g Usable Carbs.

Chocolate Mint Popsicles

by Caitlin Weeks

Low-Carb, Gluten-Free, Paleo, Vegetarian, Vegan, Nut-Free

Many times, mint is artificially derived from chemicals when used in frozen desserts. This recipe uses real mint, which gives a refreshing taste as well as antioxidant benefits. Mint is well-known for stimulating digestion, calming coughs and even soothing headaches.

Prep time: 10 minutes

Cooking time: N/A

Serves: 6 popsicles

INGREDIENTS

2 ounces unsweetened dark chocolate

2 cups full fat coconut milk, canned

¼ cup fresh mint leaves, chopped

¼ cup birch xylitol or 1 teaspoon stevia powder extract

½ cup water

PREPARATION AND INSTRUCTIONS

Melt the chocolate over medium heat in a double boiler.

Add the coconut milk, mint and water.

Let the mint simmer in the chocolate mixture for about 5 minutes for flavor.

Strain the chocolate milk mixture through a fine mesh strainer to remove the mint leaves.

Stir the sweetener and the water into the chocolate mixture and pour into the Popsicle molds.

Freeze for 6 hours.

NUTRITIONAL INFO

Serves 6; Per Serving: 155 Calories; 13.6g Fat (122 calories from fat); 55mg Cholesterol; 8mg Sodium; 1.1g Protein; 9.2g Carbohydrate; 1.8g Dietary Fiber; 7.4g Usable Carbs.

Paleo "Bread" Pudding

by Caitlin Weeks

Low-Carb, Gluten-Free, Paleo, Vegetarian, Dairy-Free, Nut-Free

The first time I had bread pudding was at a fancy steakhouse when I was about 12 years old. It is one of my best memories because it was so warm and gooey. I tried to bring back that feeling with this dish. Spaghetti squash gives this recipe a bread-like texture when cooked with egg, cream and cinnamon.

Prep time: 10 minutes

Cooking time: 30 minutes

Serves: 4

INGREDIENTS

3 cups spaghetti squash, steamed and cooled

4 eggs

⅓ cup birch xylitol or 1¼ teaspoon stevia powder extract

2 tablespoons coconut flour

½ teaspoon vanilla extract

½ cup full fat coconut milk, canned

1 teaspoon cinnamon

¼ teaspoon nutmeg

PREPARATION AND INSTRUCTIONS

Preheat the oven to 350° F.

Place all the ingredients into a food processor and pulse a few seconds until the squash is chopped but not runny.

Pour the mixture into an 8" x 8" baking dish.

Bake for 30 minutes.

Serve warm or cool from the refrigerator.

Top with Coconut Milk Whipped Cream (page 90) or heavy whipping cream as desired.

NUTRITIONAL INFO

Serves 4; Per Serving: 192 Calories; 12.5g Fat (113 calories from fat); 164mg Cholesterol; 80mg Sodium; 7.5g Protein; 13.2g Carbohydrate; 2.2g Dietary Fiber; 11g Usable Carbs.

Easy Marshmallows

by Caitlin Weeks

Low-Carb, Gluten-Free, Paleo, Dairy-Free, Nut-Free

Most marshmallow recipes are made with a lot of honey or maple syrup. It was a challenge to make them without a sugar binder. The egg whites in this recipe serve that purpose. These won't work on a stick over a campfire but they will make you feel like a kid again.

Prep time: 90 minutes

Cooking time: 5 minutes

Serves: 2

INGREDIENTS

3 tablespoons gelatin
(Great Lakes, beef, red can)

1 cup water, divided

3 eggs whites

1 teaspoon vanilla extract

¾ teaspoon stevia extract powder

PREPARATION AND INSTRUCTIONS

Mix the gelatin with ¼ cup of water and stir.

Heat up ¾ cup of water over medium heat and add the gelatin mixture.

Stir the gelatin until completely dissolved and pour it in a bowl, then stick in the freezer.

In the meantime, beat the egg whites into stiff peaks with a hand mixer.

Beat the vanilla and sweetener into the egg white mixture.

Let the gelatin cool to room temperature (but do not let it gel), then add it in a thin stream into the egg whites while beating with the hand mixer for one more minute.

Pour the mixture into a greased pie plate and chill for two hours.

Cut into squares and enjoy.

NUTRITIONAL INFO

Serves 2; Per Serving: 53 Calories; 0.1g Fat (1 calorie from fat); 0mg Cholesterol; 86mg Sodium; 8.7g Protein; 4.4g Carbohydrate; 0.6g Dietary Fiber; 3.8g Usable Carbs.

Strawberry Real Fruit Gelatin

by Caitlin Weeks

Low-Carb, Gluten-Free, Paleo, Dairy-Free, Nut-Free

Gelatin is great for achy joints and youthful skin because it is full of collagen. Make sure to get a quality brand that is made from 100% grass fed cows such as Great Lakes brand (carbsmart.com/go/gfsf-054.php). Gelatin desserts can be extremely healthy when homemade and they are a perfect treat for a low-carb diet.

Prep time: 90 minutes

Cooking time: 5 minutes

Serves: 4

INGREDIENTS

1 pound strawberries

2 cups water, divided

1 tablespoon lemon juice

¼ cup birch xylitol
or 1 teaspoon stevia powder extract

3 tablespoons gelatin
(Great Lakes beef, red can)

PREPARATION AND INSTRUCTIONS

Wash and remove the stems from the strawberries.

Place the strawberries into the food processor with 1 cup of water, lemon and sweetener.

Heat up the other cup of water over medium heat and stir in the gelatin to dissolve.

Pour the gelatin into a large bowl and let it cool for 5 minutes.

Stir the strawberry mixture into the bowl of gelatin until well combined.

Refrigerate the strawberry gelatin for one hour until cooled.

NUTRITIONAL INFO

Serves 4; Per Serving: 50 Calories; trace Fat (0.5 calories from fat); 1g Protein; 0mg Cholesterol; 4.5mg Sodium; 11g Carbohydrate; 1.6g Dietary Fiber; 9.4g Usable Carbs.

Coconut Milk Whipped Cream

by Caitlin Weeks

Low-Carb, Gluten-Free, Paleo, Vegetarian, Vegan

Many of my readers are sensitive to dairy so I wanted them to have a way to enjoy whipped cream on their desserts without having any issues. In order for coconut milk to whip it has to be drained of the water. Also make sure to use the full fat variety in a can or this recipe will not work. You can usually find the right kind of coconut milk in the Asian foods section of your grocery store.

Prep time: 5 minutes

Cooking time: N/A

Serves: 4

INGREDIENTS

1 13-ounce can full fat coconut milk

½ teaspoon vanilla

¼ teaspoon nutmeg

¼ teaspoon stevia extract powder or 2 tablespoons birch xylitol

PREPARATION AND INSTRUCTIONS

Refrigerate the can of coconut milk overnight.

The water and coconut cream should separate in the can.

Pour the water off leaving the cream.

Place the cream in a mixing bowl and whip for 5 minutes with a hand blender.

Add the vanilla, nutmeg and stevia, and then mix for another minute.

Use as a topping for treats or in coffee.

NUTRITIONAL INFO

Serves 4; Per Serving: 224 Calories; 22g Fat (198 calories from fat); 0mg Cholesterol; 14mg Sodium; 2.1g Protein; 7.7g Carbohydrate; 2.1g Dietary Fiber; 5.6g Usable Carbs.

Breakfast

They say breakfast is the most important meal of the day. Whether you're craving sweet chocolate pancakes, hot or cold cereals, or the ease of a coconut breakfast cookie, starting your day with one of our yummy breakfast treats is sure to fuel your body with all the nutrients you need for a productive day.

Sugar-Free, Grain-Free Granola

by Dana Carpender

Low-Carb, Gluten-Free, Paleo (optional), Vegetarian, Contains Nuts

Boy, did That Nice Boy I Married love this! I practically didn't need to cook supper until the granola ran out.

Prep time: 10 minutes
Cooking time: 30 minutes
Yield: 7¼ cups
Serves: 15

INGREDIENTS

2 cups flaxseed meal

2 cups shredded coconut

¾ cup vanilla whey protein powder

⅓ cup powdered Swerve

1 teaspoon cinnamon

⅓ cup coconut oil

¼ cup warm water

½ teaspoon liquid stevia extract–I like the English toffee flavor for this, but the cinnamon or the plain would work, too.

½ cup chopped pecans

½ cup sunflower seeds

½ cup chopped walnuts

½ cup sesame seeds

½ cup sliced almonds

PREPARATION AND INSTRUCTIONS

Preheat oven to 200° F.

In a big mixing bowl, combine everything from the flax seed meal through the cinnamon. Stir it up to combine.

Melt the coconut oil, then mix it (as much as possible) with the water and stevia extract. Pour this mixture into the flax/coconut mixture, and use a whisk to combine until it's all evenly dampened.

Line a big roasting pan with non-stick foil (find this with the regular foil at your grocery store) and dump the flax/coconut mixture into it. Using clean hands, press it all out into an even sheet. Put in the oven, and set a timer for 1 hour.

When the timer beeps, use the edge of your spatula to cut the flax/coconut mixture into chunks about ½" square. Scoop them up from the bottom of the pan, breaking up the clumps to your liking as you go. Now spread them out evenly in the pan again.

Sprinkle everything else evenly over the top. Slide the pan back into the oven, and set your timer for 30 minutes. When it beeps, stir it up, and give it another 30 minutes. Cool, store in a snap-top container, and use as you would any granola.

NUTRITIONAL INFO

About 15 servings of ½ cup, each with: 405 Calories; 32g Fat (66.3% calories from fat); 21g Protein; 17g Carbohydrate; 13g Dietary Fiber; 4g Usable Carbs.

Pumpkin Pancakes

by Dana Carpender

Low-Carb, Gluten-Free, Vegetarian

This delicious breakfast treat is nutrient dense with lots of protein, anti-oxidants and healthy fat.

Prep time: 5 minutes

Cooking time: 10 minutes

Serves: 4

INGREDIENTS

½ cup cottage cheese

3 eggs

1 teaspoon baking powder

½ cup canned pumpkin

½ teaspoon English Toffee liquid stevia extract

½ teaspoon salt

1½ teaspoons pumpkin pie spice

2 tablespoons granulated Swerve

¼ cup vanilla whey protein powder

¼ cup heavy cream

PREPARATION AND INSTRUCTIONS

Put your griddle or big skillet over medium heat so it will be ready to cook when your batter is ready.

Simply put all ingredients in your blender, and run until you have a smooth batter–you may need to scrape down the sides once or twice.

Cook just like regular pancakes. Make sure the bottoms are thoroughly browned before trying to flip 'em, or they'll tear.

Serve with butter, and, if you like, Swerve with cinnamon or sugar-free pancake syrup. We liked them just buttered.

NUTRITIONAL INFO

Makes a dozen pancakes–probably four servings. Each pancake will have: 65 Calories; 3g Fat (47.7% calories from fat); 6g Protein; 2g Carbohydrate; trace Dietary Fiber; 2g Usable Carbs.

Pork Rind Pancakes

by Dana Carpender

Low-Carb, Gluten-Free, Paleo (optional)

You'll think I'm crazy, but these are really good. You'd never guess what the main ingredient is! No fair feeding these to unsuspecting vegetarians, okay?

Prep time: 10 minutes

Cooking time: 10 minutes

Serves: 4

INGREDIENTS

2 ounces pork rinds. Look for pork rinds with an ingredient label that lists only "pork skins" or "pork rinds." If they say "canola oil" or "soy oil" or the like, keep looking.

3 eggs

¼ cup heavy cream or full fat coconut milk

½ teaspoon baking powder

3 tablespoons granulated Swerve

¼ teaspoon French Vanilla liquid stevia extract

½ teaspoon cinnamon

water to thin

PREPARATION AND INSTRUCTIONS

Dump your pork rinds in the food processor with the S-blade in place, and run until they're reduced to fine crumbs.

In a mixing bowl, whisk together the eggs, cream, baking powder, Swerve, stevia, and cinnamon. Now add the pork rind crumbs and whisk them in.

Let the batter sit for 10 minutes or so. During this time it will "gloppify"–thicken up and become gloppy. That's okay!

While you're waiting for the gloppification to occur, put your skillet or griddle over medium-high heat. You'll want it hot for frying your pancakes.

Thin your batter with water if you like–just depends on how thick a pancake you want. Then fry like any other pancake batter. I scoop my batter with a cookie scoop–like an ice cream scoop, only smaller–so they all come out the same size.

Serve with sugar-free pancake syrup, Swerve with cinnamon, or sugar-free low-carb preserves–Polaner makes an excellent version in several flavors.

NUTRITIONAL INFO

8 really filling pancakes, each with: 89 Calories; 7g Fat (67.6% calories from fat); 7g Protein; 1g Carbohydrate; trace Dietary Fiber.

NOTES

The brand of pork rinds matters here. You want a brand that's quite fluffy, rather than super-crunchy, and you want them to not be too heavily salted. And obviously, you don't want the barbecue flavored ones!

Chia "Oatmeal"

by Caitlin Weeks

Low-Carb, Gluten-Free, Paleo, Vegetarian, Vegan, Nut-Free

Chia seeds come from Central America and they make their own gel when put into water. They contain Omega-3 but it is not very well absorbed in humans when coming from a plant source.

Prep time: 10 minutes

Cooking time: 5 minutes

Serves: 2

INGREDIENTS

1 cup boiling water

¼ cup chia seeds

½ cup full fat coconut milk, canned

¾ cup pumpkin, canned

¼ cup shredded coconut

½ teaspoon cinnamon

½ teaspoon nutmeg

½ teaspoon stevia powder extract

2 tablespoons ground flaxseed meal

PREPARATION AND INSTRUCTIONS

Mix the boiling water and the chia and let it sit for 10 minutes or until it gels.

In a saucepan over medium heat, mix the coconut milk, pumpkin, coconut shreds, cinnamon, nutmeg, and stevia.

Once the pumpkin mixture is warm, remove from heat and add in the chia and flax. Pour the mixture into bowls and enjoy.

NUTRITIONAL INFO

Serves 2; Per Serving: 337 Calories; 29.1g Fat (262 calories from fat); 0mg Cholesterol; 20mg Sodium; 7.5g Protein; 21.4g Carbohydrate; 12.3g Dietary Fiber; 9.1g Usable Carbs.

Choco Pancakes with Chocolate Syrup

by Caitlin Weeks

Low-Carb, Gluten-Free, Paleo, Vegetarian, Nut-Free

I love chocolate and pancakes so I thought why not put them all together. These pancakes will hit the spot on a slow Sunday morning while reading the funny papers. Sop up with the guilt-free chocolate syrup with each chewy bite.

Prep time: 5 minutes

Cooking time: 15 minutes

Serves: 2; makes 6-8 pancakes

CHOCO PANCAKES INGREDIENTS

6 eggs

¾ cup full fat coconut milk, canned

¼ teaspoon stevia powder extract

4 tablespoons coconut flour

4 tablespoons cocoa powder

¼ teaspoon sea salt

½ teaspoon baking soda

1 tablespoon coconut oil for frying

CHOCO PANCAKES PREPARATION AND INSTRUCTIONS

Mix the eggs and coconut milk with sweetener in one bowl.

Sift the coconut flour and cocoa powder into a bowl with the salt and baking soda. Combine the two mixtures and stir

Heat up a frying pan and melt the coconut oil.

Spoon ¼ cup of the batter in the pan and cook for a few minutes on each side.

Repeat until all the batter is cooked.

Top with melted butter, whip cream, or chocolate syrup (see recipe below) as desired.

CHOCOLATE SYRUP INGREDIENTS

4 tablespoons butter

2 tablespoons cocoa powder

½ teaspoon stevia powder extract

CHOCOLATE SYRUP PREPARATION AND INSTRUCTIONS

Melt butter and add cocoa powder over medium heat.

Add stevia powder extract and stir.

Pour over pancakes. Adds 2 net carbs.

NUTRITIONAL INFO

Serves 2; 3-4 pancakes Per Serving: 518 Calories; 41.4g Fat (373 calories from fat); 0mg Cholesterol; 595mg Sodium; 23.3g Protein; 17.3g Carbohydrate; 8.2g Dietary Fiber; 9.1g Usable Carbs.

Egg-Free Coconut Breakfast Cookie

by Caitlin Weeks

Low-Carb, Gluten-Free, Paleo, Egg-Free, Vegetarian, Vegan

I took these to my friend Mary who is also a nutritionist. She has an egg sensitivity so she was so grateful to have a cookie without eggs. These are great as a snack or as a healthy breakfast option.

Prep time: 10 minutes

Cooking time: 15 minutes

Serves: 12 cookies

INGREDIENTS

3 tablespoons chia seeds

9 tablespoons water

¼ cup coconut flour

½ cup birch xylitol
or 2 teaspoon stevia powder extract

¾ shredded coconut, unsweetened

½ teaspoon baking soda

½ teaspoon sea salt

¾ cup coconut butter (I suggest Nutiva Coconut Manna brand)

½ teaspoon vanilla extract

PREPARATION AND INSTRUCTIONS

Preheat the oven to 350° F.

Grind the chia seeds in a coffee grinder until it becomes a fine powder and then mix with the water.

Let the chia mixture gel, about 10 minutes.

Sift the coconut flour into a separate bowl.

Mix the sweetener, shredded coconut, baking soda and salt with the coconut flour.

Melt the coconut butter over medium heat with the vanilla.

Combine the coconut butter mixture with the dry ingredients and stir well.

Add the chia gel to the dough and mix well with your hands.

Roll the cookie dough into 1-inch balls and place on a cookie sheet covered in parchment paper.

Bake for 15-18 minutes until browned.

NUTRITIONAL INFO

Serves 12; Per Serving (1 cookie): 209 Calories; 18.3g Fat (164 calories from fat); 0mg Cholesterol; 141mg Sodium; 2.7g Protein; 11g Carbohydrate; 6.2g Dietary Fiber; 4.8g Usable Carbs.

Easy Cinnamon Granola

by Caitlin Weeks

Low-Carb, Gluten-Free, Paleo, Vegetarian, Vegan, Contains Nuts

I made this granola for my dad who is new to the low-carb lifestyle. He was so happy to have something healthy while he was transitioning away from eating toast for breakfast. Just add some almond milk to this granola for cereal or bag it to go on a hike.

Prep time: 8 hours
Cooking time: 30 minutes
Serves: 8

INGREDIENTS

1 cup sunflower seeds

1 cup shelled pumpkin seeds

1 cup sliced almonds

1 cup shredded coconut

1 teaspoon nutmeg

2 teaspoon cinnamon

1 teaspoon sea salt

¼ cup birch xylitol
or 1 teaspoon powdered stevia extract

1 cup dried unsweetened cranberries

¼ cup coconut oil, melted

PREPARATION AND INSTRUCTIONS

Soak the sunflower and pumpkin seeds overnight.

Drain the seeds and dry on a paper towel for 15 minutes.

Preheat the oven to 300° F.

Add all nuts, seeds, shredded coconut, spices, salt, sweetener, and cranberries to a large bowl.

Add the melted coconut oil to the bowl and stir to coat.

Pour the mixture out into a cookie sheet lined with parchment paper.

Cook for 20 minutes, stirring every 5 minutes to avoid burning.

Let the mixture cool for 45 minutes then place in airtight container.

Serve with coconut milk or almond milk and eat like cereal or just eat with your hands as a snack.

NUTRITIONAL INFO

Serves 8; 1.5 cups Per Serving: 345 Calories; 31.7g Fat (285 calories from fat); 82mg Cholesterol; 242mg Sodium; 9.6g Protein; 14.6g Carbohydrate; 6.4g Dietary Fiber; 8.2g Usable Carbs.

Breads, Crackers, and Muffins

Thought you couldn't have bread on your low-carb or Paleo diet? Think again. Whether you choose sweet or savory, all our mouth-watering recipes are guaranteed sugar-free and grain-free. We promise that your friends won't be able to the difference!

Parmesan Garlic Bread

by Dana Carpender

Low-Carb, Gluten-Free, Vegetarian, Contains Nuts

Yes, Parmesan Garlic Bread. It doesn't get much better than this! Serve this bread with a large bowl of zucchini pasta topped with roasted veggies for a delicious meal the whole family will love.

Prep time: 15-20 minutes
Cooking time: 2 hours
Serves: 20

INGREDIENTS

3 cups shredded coconut meat
–the finely shredded stuff, not the big flakes

1 cup almond meal

¾ cup flaxseed meal

3 tablespoons gluten-free xanthan gum

2 teaspoons baking soda

½ teaspoon salt

1 cup grated Parmesan cheese–I used the cheap stuff in the green shaker

2 cloves garlic, crushed

2 teaspoons Italian seasoning

5 eggs

½ cup water

2 tablespoons apple cider vinegar

PREPARATION AND INSTRUCTIONS

Preheat oven to 350° F. Unless you have a really good non-stick loaf pan, line a loaf pan with non-stick foil.

Dump your coconut in the food processor, and run it for about five minutes, until the coconut is reduced to a fine meal. Add the almond meal, flaxseed meal, xanthan gum, baking soda, and salt, and run for another few minutes.

Add the Parmesan, garlic, and Italian seasoning, and once again run the processor for a minute or two, making sure everything is well-blended.

Now add the eggs and run the processor until they're completely blended in.

Mix the water and vinegar. With the processor running, slowly pour the vinegar-water in–if you have to stop and scrape down the sides to get an even mixture, do it, but work fast; once you add the vinegar to the mixture the clock is ticking. Don't run the processor any longer than you have to get an even mixture.

Turn your dough/batter out into the loaf pan, and use a rubber scraper to spread it evenly.

Put the bread in your PREHEATED oven–that the oven is already up to temperature is important–and bake for 2 hours. Yes, 2 hours–if it's underdone in the middle, you'll have to put it back in and bake it some more, and it's not as good.

Turn out of the pan onto a wire rack to cool, then slice and eat like any bread. Especially good toasted with butter and mozzarella on top.

NUTRITIONAL INFO

20 slices, each with: 147 Calories; 11g Fat (61.0% calories from fat); 8g Protein; 7g Carbohydrate; 4g Dietary Fiber; 3g Usable Carbs.

Nacho Cheese Crackers

by Dana Carpender

Low-Carb, Gluten-Free, Vegetarian, Nut-Free

Wow. Just...wow. Didn't think you could enjoy a delicious tasting cracker on your low-carb, Paleo, or gluten-free lifestyle? Think again! These crackers are not only tasty but chock full of healthy ingredients.

Prep time: 15 minutes
Cooking time: 25-30 minutes
Yields 6 dozen

INGREDIENTS

1½ cups sunflower seeds, raw, shelled

1½ cups shredded cheddar cheese, sharp

¼ teaspoon baking powder

1½ teaspoons onion powder

1½ teaspoons garlic powder

½ teaspoon cayenne, or to taste

½ teaspoon salt, plus more for sprinkling

¼ cup water

PREPARATION AND INSTRUCTIONS

Pre-heat your oven to 350° F.

In your food processor, using the S-blade, grind your sunflower seeds to a fine meal. Now add the cheddar, baking powder, and seasonings, and run until you have a uniform mixture.

With the processor running, drizzle in the water. You'll wind up with a soft, sticky dough.

Line a cookie sheet with baking parchment. (WARNING: DO NOT SKIP THE BAKING PARCHMENT. YOU WILL REGRET IT.) Take about half the dough and put it on the lined cookie sheet, then lay another sheet of parchment over it. Use your rolling pin to roll the dough out as thinly and evenly as possible–so long as there are no holes, the thinner, the better.

Peel off the top piece of parchment, and use a long, thin, straight-bladed (as opposed to serrated) knife to score into squares or diamonds–I make mine roughly the size of Wheat Thins. The tidiest way to score the crackers, by the way, is to put the whole edge of the blade down on the crackers, and press down. This works a lot better than slicing. Sprinkle your crackers with salt to taste.

Bake the crackers for 25-30 minutes, but start checking at 20. You may roll yours thinner than I do, and you don't want them to scorch. While they're baking, roll out the other half of the dough.

Let 'em cool on the parchment, then peel them off and break along the scored lines. Store in a snap-top container or cookie can.

NUTRITIONAL INFO

I got 6 dozen, each with: 27 Calories; 2g Fat (72.2% calories from fat); 1g Protein; 1g Carbohydrate; trace Dietary Fiber; 1g Usable Carb.

NOTES

If you decide you like making crackers, do yourself a favor: Run to the housewares store or Amazon.com and buy a set of rolling pin rings (carbsmart.com/go/gfsf-064.php). These are rings of silicone in varying thicknesses that you put around either end of your rolling pin. This allows you to easily roll your dough out into an even sheet. I use the thinnest rings in my set for making crackers.

Swiss Almond Crackers

by Dana Carpender

Low-Carb, Gluten-Free, Vegetarian, Contains Nuts

Enjoy these crunchy crackers with dips, sliced salmon, or by themselves. They won't disappoint!

Prep time: 10 minutes

Cooking time: 20-25 minutes

Yields: 4 dozen

INGREDIENTS

1 cup almond meal

½ teaspoon salt, plus more for sprinkling

½ teaspoon baking powder

2 teaspoons gluten-free xanthan gum

1 cup shredded Swiss cheese

1 egg white

1 tablespoon water

PREPARATION AND INSTRUCTIONS

Preheat oven to 350° F.

In your food processor, using the S-blade, combine the almond meal with the salt, baking powder, and xanthan gum, and run for a few seconds to distribute them evenly.

Now add your shredded Swiss cheese, and pulse the processor until it's evenly blended with the sunflower meal.

With the processor running, add your egg white (I give the yolk to the dog). Keep it running, and add the water. You'll have a nice dough when it's blended in.

Follow the directions under Nacho Cheese Crackers (page 101) to roll and cut the crackers–and again, DO NOT SKIP THE PARCHMENT. Sprinkle with salt, and bake for about 20-25 minutes, or until lightly browned. Cool on cookie sheets, then peel off parchment and break apart.

NUTRITIONAL INFO

I got 4 dozen, each with: 20 Calories; 1g Fat (48.5% calories from fat); 2g Protein; 1g Carbohydrate; 0g Dietary Fiber; 1g Usable Carb.

Cocoa Pumpkin Bread

by Caitlin Weeks

Low-Carb, Gluten-Free, Paleo, Vegetarian, Dairy-Free, Nut-Free

I love pumpkin because it's low in carbs and full of fiber. Cocoa powder has magnesium which is helpful for over 300 bodily processes. When these ingredients are combined with healthy fats and protein it creates a super food "bread" loaf.

Prep time: 10 minutes

Cooking time: 30 minutes

Serves: 4 (makes 1 loaf)

INGREDIENTS

4 eggs

1 cup canned pumpkin

2 tablespoons coconut oil, melted

2 tablespoons coconut flour

4 tablespoons cocoa powder

1 pinch salt

½ teaspoon baking soda

1 teaspoon stevia powder extract
or ¼ cup birch xylitol

PREPARATION AND INSTRUCTIONS

Mix the wet ingredients.

Sift the dry ingredients into another bowl and mix.

Combine the two mixtures.

Pour into a greased bread pan.

Bake for 30 minutes.

VARIATIONS

Get creative. Instead of using a bread pan, bake in a casserole dish, muffin tins or ramekins!

NUTRITIONAL INFO

Serves 4; Per Serving: 174 Calories; 12.6g Fat (113 calories from fat); 164mg Cholesterol; 264mg Sodium; 7.9g Protein; 10.3g Carbohydrate; 4.6g Dietary Fiber; 5.7g Usable Carbs.

"Cornbread" Biscuits

by Caitlin Weeks

Low-Carb, Gluten-Free, Paleo, Vegetarian, Nut-Free, (Vegan if using palm shortening)

Nutritional yeast is an ingredient that was popular in the 1970's. Many people used it on popcorn because it has a cheesy taste. It is full of B vitamins and is a good dairy substitute for those who are intolerant. The yeast in these biscuits makes them taste similar to cornbread.

Prep time: 10 minutes

Cooking time: 50 minutes

Serves: 6 (makes 6 biscuits)

INGREDIENTS

4 tablespoons coconut flour

¼ cup nutritional yeast
(carbsmart.com/go/gfsf-065.php)–Foods Alive is best for non-gmo and gluten-free)

⅓ cup palm shortening
or softened butter

4 eggs

¼ teaspoon pepper

½ teaspoon baking soda

PREPARATION AND INSTRUCTIONS

Preheat the oven to 350° F.

Mix all the ingredients with a whisk.

Place the batter on a baking sheet lined with parchment paper in 2-inch circles.

Bake for 15 minutes.

Cool and enjoy!

NUTRITIONAL INFO

Serves 6; Per Serving: 193 Calories; 15.3g Fat (138 calories from fat); 109mg Cholesterol; 151mg Sodium; 7.8g Protein; 6g Carbohydrate; 3.4g Dietary Fiber; 2.6g Usable Carbs.

Coconut Flax Chia Bread

by Dana Carpender

Low-Carb, Gluten-Free, Paleo, Ketogenic, Vegetarian

My original recipe for coconut-flax bread called for xanthan gum or guar gum to add structure and make it slice without crumbling. Here, chia seeds serve the same purpose, but also add some omega-3 fats.

Prep time: 10 minutes
Cooking time: 75 minutes
Serves: 20

INGREDIENTS

4 cups shredded coconut meat

½ cup flaxseed meal

2 tablespoons chia seeds

1½ teaspoons baking soda

1 teaspoon erythritol
(carbsmart.com/go/gfsf-024.php)

½ teaspoon salt

½ cup water

2 tablespoons cider vinegar

4 eggs

PREPARATION AND INSTRUCTIONS

Preheat oven to 350° F. Grease a standard-size loaf pan, or line it with non-stick foil (I use the foil).

Put the coconut, flax meal, chia seeds, baking soda, erythritol, and salt in your food processor, and run it until it's thoroughly ground up–we're talking at least 5 minutes, and perhaps as long as 10. Stop the processor and scrape down the sides from time to time during this process.

While the processor is running, measure the water in a measuring cup with a pouring lip, and add the vinegar to it.

When the mixture in the food processor is super-well-ground (you'll still see individual chia seeds), leave the machine running and start adding the eggs, one at a time, through the feed shoot. Again, stop and scrape down the sides once or twice if you need to get an even mixture.

After all the eggs are in, slowly pour in the water/vinegar combo. You will wind up with a thick batter.

Immediately spread this batter in your prepared loaf pan, and bake for 1 hour 15 minutes–depending on your oven and the size of your loaf pan you may decide 90 minutes is better.

Remove from the pan and cool on a wire rack. Store in a zipper-lock bag in the refrigerator. Slice and spread with butter, cream cheese, whatever you like. This recipe toasts well, too.

NUTRITIONAL INFO

20 slices, each with: 104 Calories; 9g Fat (70.3% calories from fat); 3g Protein; 5g Carbohydrate; 4g Dietary Fiber; 1g Usable Carb.

Acknowledgements

A cookbook like this does not get completed without a great team. What I like about creating these cookbooks most is that I have a team of great friends to work with.

Dana Carpender has been a friend since 1999 when we sold her first independently produced book How I Gave Up My Low-Fat Diet and Lost 40 Pounds (carbsmart.com/go/gfsf-068.php) at CarbSmart.com. Dana inspires me daily to try new recipes (most of them hers) that keep me on my ketogenic lifestyle.

I met **Caitlin Weeks** when she was an attendee on the 2012 Low-Carb Cruise. I had visited her GrassFedGirl.com web site many times and knew she was a wonderful writer but getting to know her taught me that her transformational story made her an even bigger inspiration to her many, many readers including myself. Her articles at CarbSmart.com (carbsmart.com/go/gfsf-008.php) continue to inspire and help many adopt a cleaner lifestyle.

Marcy Guyer has been my right-hand (wo)man for years and I couldn't run CarbSmart without her. Thanks for taking all the crap I throw at you and making it into something so much better.

Jeff Guyer is an amazing photographer but more importantly he is an amazing father to an amazing son. He also gives Marcy (his wife) the ability to help make CarbSmart better with her wonderful ideas and continuous participation.

Amy Dungan was first a success story on CarbSmart.com (carbsmart.com/go/gfsf-069.php) in 2003. She took that success and started helping thousands of readers at her popular Healthy Low-Carb Living website (carbsmart.com/go/gfsf-070.php). Being a wife and mother, avid photographer, and amazing writer makes Amy an invaluable member of this team.

Cassie Bjork is a woman who gets it. She is known world wide as Dietitian Cassie, a trained dietitian that helps others change their life with a low-carb lifestyle. Whether she is posting recipes and articles at <u>DietitianCassie.com</u> or podcasting with Jimmy Moore at <u>LowCarbConversations.com</u>, Cassie is leading the discussion on proper low-carb health.

Carolyn Ketchum from <u>AllDayIDreamAboutFood.com</u> is one of the best low-carb recipe creators and bloggers and did an amazing job proofreading this cookbook. Watch for many great things to come from her in the future.

John Furkin is not only a graphic superstar, he is a dedicated professional. You ask him to do a basic design and he gives you a spectacular, well-thought-out design. You ask him to do a project as fast as possible and he still takes the time to proof your work and finds errors 12 other people should have found before it got to him. Thank you John, for your attention to detail and for being you.

Thank you team!

Andrew DiMino
President, Publisher, and Founder
CarbSmart, Inc.

Resources

Online Resources

We have created an entire resource section as easy-to-use lists.

Grain-Free, Sugar-Free ingredients list at CarbSmart.com:
carbsmart.com/go/gfsf-085.php

Grain-Free, Sugar-Free ingredients list at Amazon.com:
carbsmart.com/go/gfsf-001.php

Grain-Free, Sugar-Free ingredients list at NevadaManna.com:
carbsmart.com/go/gfsf-080.php

CarbSmart.com
(carbsmart.com) – if you have friends or relatives who live a low-carbohydrate, diabetic, or Paleo lifestyle, you'll want to introduce them to our sister web site. CarbSmart.com is your trusted guide to the low-carb lifestyle and includes thousands of articles and product reviews to help people lower their blood sugar, control their weight, and possibly reduce or eliminate the risk of pre-diabetes or diabetes. This is accomplished mostly through choosing a healthy lifestyle without sugar, wheat or most unnecessary carbohydrates.

Fat Fast Cookbook
(carbsmart.com/go/gfsf-051.php) – Our bestselling cookbook from Dana Carpender, Amy Dungan, and Rebecca Latham. Jump-Start Your Low-Carb Weight Loss with Fat Fast Cookbook! Are you having trouble losing weight, even on the Atkins Induction phase? Have you lost weight successfully on low-carb, but hit a plateau or started to regain weight even though you're still following your low-carb diet? Are you looking for a way to add more healthy fat to your low-carb diet? If you suspect you've been doing something wrong, we've got your solution. Introducing your new low-carb weight loss tools: The Fat Fast and Nutritional Ketosis.

GlutenSmart.com
(glutensmart.com) – our main web site. Here you'll find the latest news and information to help you live a gluten-free lifestyle. You'll also find product reviews, recipes, and other resources to keep you gluten-free and healthy.

Easy Gluten-Free Entertaining
(carbsmart.com/go/gfsf-067.php) – From our sister web site, 50+ recipes your guests won't know are gluten-free but will love! Whether you're hosting a small intimate gathering of friends or a large party with an open guest list, Easy Gluten-Free

Entertaining will satisfy everyone whether they live gluten-free or not. Inside you'll be treated to practically limitless recipe and menu ideas safe for anyone eliminating wheat or gluten from their daily lives. Not only are all these recipes gluten-free, most of them are also grain-free, nut-free, dairy-free, vegetarian, and/or vegan.

Online Retailers

Amazon.com
(carbsmart.com/go/gfsf-001.php) – They're not called the world's largest retailer for no reason. Not only can you find any of the ingredients you need from this cookbook, you can find just about everything else you need from electronics to clothing.

Netrition.com
(carbsmart.com/go/gfsf-005.php) – A low-carb dieter's best friend, Netrition has been a retailer of ingredients and prepackaged foods for low carbers since 1998.

Vitacost.com
(carbsmart.com/go/gfsf-vitacost.php) – Since 1999, Vitacost has been one of the largest health foods and vitamin retailers in the world. Expect fast shipping from their two warehouses.

MountainRoseHerbs.com
(carbsmart.com/go/gfsf-006.php) – Since 1987, Mountain Rose Herbs has been known for exceptional quality certified organic bulk herbs and spices with a strict emphasis on sustainable agriculture.

Penzeys.com
(carbsmart.com/go/gfsf-007.php) – Penzey's has a marvelous reputation for fresh spices. See why their unmatched quality, abundant variety, and love of everyone who cooks have made them the top on-line seller of spices.

Ingredients

SweetLeaf Sweet Drops
Liquid Stevia Extract 2.0 oz.
(carbsmart.com/go/gfsf-016.php) – Made with stevia leaf extract and natural flavors, add to foods or beverages–for sweet, sugar-free flavor in your ketogenic recipes. Available in 17 flavors including:

SweetLeaf SteviaClear
(carbsmart.com/go/gfsf-078.php)

SweetLeaf Vanilla Crème
(carbsmart.com/go/gfsf-012.php)

SweetLeaf Chocolate
(carbsmart.com/go/gfsf-013.php)

SweetLeaf English Toffee
(carbsmart.com/go/gfsf-014.php)

SweetLeaf Lemon Drop
(carbsmart.com/go/gfsf-015.php)

Health Garden
Kosher Birch Xylitol 16 oz.
(carbsmart.com/go/gfsf-045.php) – Xylitol made in the USA from real birch, not corn. Its granulated crystals and lack of bitter after taste make it perfect for all of your baking needs.

Xyla Birch Xylitol
(carbsmart.com/go/gfsf-028.php) – North American Birch Xylitol Powder is a 1 to 1 or "cup for cup" sweetness compared to table sugar. Use as a replacement in any recipe.

SweetLeaf
Organic Stevia Extract Powder 0.9 oz.
(carbsmart.com/go/gfsf-046.php) – 100% pure stevia leaf extract with a minimum 90% steviosides. use for baking and cooking. ¼ teaspoon is equivalent to 1 cup of sugar.

Dried Stevia Leaf
(carbsmart.com/go/gfsf-023.php) – 100% dried Stevia leaves. Tested by Anresco Labs in San Francisco, for pesticide and chemical free assurance.

Swerve Granular Sweetener 16 oz.
(carbsmart.com/go/gfsf-023.php) – Swerve is a great tasting, natural sweetener that measures cup-for-cup just like sugar! Made from a unique combination of ingredients derived from fruits and vegetables, Swerve contains no artificial ingredients, preservatives or flavors. Swerve is non-glycemic and safe for those living with diabetes. Contains erythritol, oligosacchardies and natural flavor.

Swerve Powdered Sweetener 16 oz.
(carbsmart.com/go/gfsf-027.php) – With Confectioners Style (powdered) Swerve, even cupcake frosting can be guilt-free! Contains erythritol, oligosacchardies and natural flavor.

EZ-Sweetz Liquid Stevia
(carbsmart.com/go/gfsf-021.php) – EZ-Sweetz Stevia is a liquid sweetener made from Stevia extract. The proprietary blend offers no unpleasant aftertaste and none of the characteristic bitterness of Stevia. Best of all, this sweetener has absolutely no calories or carbohydrates!

EZ-Sweetz Liquid Stevia/Monk fruit
Blend (carbsmart.com/go/gfsf-022.php) – EZ-Sweetz Stevia & Monk Fruit is a new liquid sweetener made from the extracts of Stevia leaves and a sweet melon called monk fruit. The synergy of this proprietary blend means it has no unpleasant aftertaste and has a clean, slightly caramel-y taste similar to raw sugar, with none of the characteristic bitterness of Stevia. Best of all, this new sweetener has absolutely no calories and no carbohydrates!

Yacon Syrup Natural Sweetener
(carbsmart.com/go/gfsf-029.php) – Pure yacon syrup is Paleo-friendly and assists in weight loss by regulating blood sugar, and increasing daily fiber intake. The syrup, distilled from the Peruvian tuber yacon, contains up to 50 percent fructooligosacharides, or FOS. FOS, classified as a prebiotic, is a non-caloric sweetener and also a fiber source.

Bob's Red Mill Chia Seeds
(carbsmart.com/go/gfsf-030.php)
– A recent ingredient for low-carb and
Paleo recipes, Chia seed originated in
South America and was a staple in the
diets of ancient Mayans and Aztecs.
The tiny seeds of the chia plant can be
eaten right out of the bag, sprinkled
on hot cereal and used in baking, for
a nutritional boost comparable only to
flaxseed in Omega 3 and dietary fiber
content.

Bob's Red Mill Finely Ground Natural
Almond Meal 16 oz.
(carbsmart.com/go/gfsf-031.php) – Made
from blanched whole almonds, Almonds
Meal/Flour is simply skinless, blanched
almonds that have been finely ground. It
lends a moist texture and rich, buttery
flavor to low-carb cakes, cookies, muffins,
breads and a host of other desserts.

Bob's Red Mill Coconut Flour 16 oz.
(carbsmart.com/go/gfsf-032.php)
– Coconut flour is a delicious, healthy
alternative to wheat and other grain flours.
It is very high in fiber, low in digestible
carbohydrates, a good source of protein
and gluten-free. It lends baked goods an
incomparably rich texture and a unique,
natural sweetness.

Bob's Red Mill Flaxseed Meal 16 oz.
(carbsmart.com/go/gfsf-033.php)
– Flaxseed meal has a robust, nutty flavor
and tastes really great. Two tablespoons
added to your cold or hot low-carb cereals,
pancakes and waffles or baked into your
breads, muffins and quick breads brings
you amazing nutrition.

Bob's Red Mill Sunflower Seeds
(carbsmart.com/go/gfsf-038.php)
– Sunflower seeds are delicious as a
high protein snack and as an ingredient
for low-carb bread, cakes, cookies
and muffins. They are also a crunchy
substitute for bacon bits and croutons on
cooked vegetables and salads.

Tera's Whey Grass-Fed
Organic Bourbon Vanilla 12 oz.
(carbsmart.com/go/gfsf-074.php) – This
is an amazing grass-fed, organic whey
protein powder that Caitlin recommends.
Grass-fed, organic, and no artificial
sweeteners or any additional flavors.

Ultimate Natural Whey Protein
(carbsmart.com/go/gfsf-081.php)
– Premium protein powder recommended
by Dietitian Cassie Bjork. This protein
powder is imported from New Zealand
where rBGH is not approved for use–it has
no artificial sweeteners or added sugars
and it mixes really well.

Let's Do Organic
Unsweetened Shredded Coconut 8 oz.
(carbsmart.com/go/gfsf-036.php) – Finely
shredded coconut for baking. zero grams
of sugar with no sulfites or preservatives.
100% organic.

Let's Do Organic Coconut Flakes 7 oz.
(carbsmart.com/go/gfsf-037.php)
– Ideal for low-carb and Paleo baking,
desserts, and making granola.

MCT oil (carbsmart.com/go/gfsf-039.php)
– The ketogenic wonder oil, MCT Oil is
perfect in high-fat, low-carb recipes.

San-J Tamari Black Label
Gluten-Free Soy Sauce
(carbsmart.com/go/gfsf-040.php) – This organic wheat-free tamari is certified by Quality Assurance International (QAI). It is made with 100% soybeans and no wheat. It is naturally fermented for up to 6 months. San-J does not add MSG or any artificial preservatives. Their fermentation process is different from that of ordinary soy sauce, giving it unique flavor enhancing properties.

Coconut Secret Raw Organic Vegan
Coconut Aminos 8 oz.
(carbsmart.com/go/gfsf-041.php)
– A soy-free soy sauce alternative, organic, gluten-free, dairy-free, and vegan coconut aminos is raw, very low glycemic, an and abundant source of 17 amino acids, minerals, vitamin and has a nearly neutral pH.

Konriko Creole Seasoning 6 oz.
(carbsmart.com/go/gfsf-043.php) – For a quick, clean Creole seasoning, Konriko's will provide that Cajun kick without the carbs.

Great Lakes Gelatin, Collagen
Hydrolysate (green can)
(carbsmart.com/go/gfsf-044.php) – Great for liquid recipes, hydrolyzed collagen helps regulate the body's metabolism by providing pure protein of low molecular weight that is quickly absorbed in the digestive track. The rapid absorption and distinctive amino acid groups in this formula will positively impact a large number of metabolic pathways.

Great Lakes
Unflavored Beef Gelatin (orange can)
(carbsmart.com/go/gfsf-054.php) – Beef gelatin is perfect in regular and low-carb recipes. Pure protein and Kosher, Great Lakes Gelatin is so much better than those other cheap brands.

Hershey's Sugar-Free
Chocolate Chip Baking Chips
(carbsmart.com/go/gfsf-048.php) – These taste and bake like regular chocolate chips–but without the sugar. These low-carb chocolate chips do have maltitol in them so use them carefully.

Equal Exchange
Semi-Sweet Chocolate Chips
(carbsmart.com/go/gfsf-075.php) – Vegan, soy and gluten-free (not sugar-free or low-carb though–great for a Paleo lifestyle though), Use these delicious organic chocolate chips to add something special to cookies, brownies and even pancakes. Pair with our organic baking cocoa for even more chocolaty goodness in your favorite chocolate recipes. Made with organic and fairly traded cacao from small-scale farmers in Peru, and sugar from small-scale farmers in Paraguay.

Nutiva Certified Organic Extra Virgin
Coconut Oil
(carbsmart.com/go/gfsf-050.php) – A deliciously healthy cooking oil that's low-carb, gluten-free and ketogenic. Better than butter in so many ways. Unrefined with no trans fats.

Nutiva Organic Coconut Manna
(carbsmart.com/go/gfsf-063.php) – Pure coconut cream which is a staple of low-carb and Paleo baking.

Native Forest
Organic Classic Coconut Milk
(carbsmart.com/go/gfsf-053.php) – A staple of Thai, Indian and Caribbean cuisines, full fat Coconut Milk imparts rich and creamy goodness to wonderful low-carb, gluten-free, and Paleo dishes.

Mauna Loa Macadamia Nuts
(carbsmart.com/go/gfsf-075.php) – Macadamia nuts were Dr. Atkins' favorite snack! Low-carb macadamia nuts can be eaten any time or crushed up and used in your favorite ketogenic baking.

Farmer's Market Foods
Organic Canned Pumpkin
(carbsmart.com/go/gfsf-058.php) – Organic pumpkin is rich, smooth and delicious, and ready to use for everything from low-carb baked delights to savory center of the plate entrees. Use it in a variety of low-carb recipes including pies, muffins, cookies, and soups.

Spectrum Organic Shortening
(carbsmart.com/go/gfsf-073.php) – Made with organic palm oil, Spectrum Organic Shortening is a healthy, trans-fat free alternative to traditional shortening for flaky crusts and Paleo-friendly creations.

The Authors

Dana Carpender   Caitlin Weeks, NC

Dana Carpender

In retrospect, Dana Carpender's career seems inevitable: She's been cooking since she had to stand on a step stool to reach the stove. She was also a dangerously sugar-addicted child, eventually stealing from her parents to support her habit, and was in Weight Watchers by age 11. At 19 Dana read her first book on nutrition, and recognized herself in a list of symptoms of reactive hypoglycemia. She ditched sugar and white flour, and was dazzled by the near-instantaneous improvement in her physical and mental health. A lifetime nutrition buff was born.

Unfortunately, in the late '80s and early '90s, Dana got sucked into low-fat/high carb mania, and whole-grain-and-beaned her way up to a size 20, with nasty energy swings, constant hunger, and borderline high blood pressure. In 1995, she read a nutrition book from the 1950s that stated that obesity had nothing to do with how much one ate, but was rather a carbohydrate intolerance disease. She thought, "What the heck, might as well give it a try." Three days later her clothes were loose, her hunger was gone, and her energy level was through the roof. She never looked back, and has now been low-carb for 19 years and counting– $1/3$ of her life.

Realizing that this change was permanent, and being a cook at heart, Dana set about creating as varied and satisfying a cuisine as she could with a minimal carb load. And being an enthusiastic, gregarious sort, she started sharing her experience. By 1997 she was writing about it. The upshot is

over 2,500 recipes published, and more than a million books sold–and she still has ideas left to try! Dana lives in Bloomington, Indiana with her husband, three dogs, and a cat, all of whom are well and healthily fed.

Website: HoldTheToast.com

Facebook:facebook.com/pages/ Dana-Carpenders-Hold-The-Toast-Press/118433594850660

Twitter: twitter.com/danacarpender

Caitlin Weeks, NC

Caitlin Weeks BA, NC, CPT is a full time blogger at GrassFedGirl.com. She is an author who co-wrote Mediterranean Paleo Cooking (carbsmart.com/go/gfsf-084.php) with her husband, chef Nabil Boumrar. She has many years of experience as a Certified Nutrition Consultant, C.H.E.K. Holistic Lifestyle Coach, and professional personal trainer in San Francisco, CA.

Caitlin has had success conquering obesity after a lifelong struggle with her weight. Since 2009 she has been winning the battle against Hashimoto's Thyroiditis using a Paleo diet. She truly believes in the mind- body connection for healing and is certified EFT practitioner. She is committed to educating others about the benefits of traditional/ancestral foods and efficient exercise.

Website: GrassFedGirl.com

Facebook: facebook.com/Grassfedgirl

Twitter: twitter.com/grassfedgirlsf

Instagram: instagram.com/grassfedgirl

Pinterest: pinterest.com/grassfedgirl

Caitlin's Mediterranean Paleo Cooking Cookbook (carbsmart.com/go/gfsf-084.php)

Made in the USA
San Bernardino, CA
05 May 2016